"*Bake It Vegan* is a great example of how simple, joyful and creative vegan baking can be."

—TIINA STRANDBERG, creator of My Berry Forest

"Maja's recipes and her focus on whole, healthy and delicious eating have always been a huge hit with my family. Can't wait to try all her new decadent dessert recipes!"

— MITRA SHIR, MSC, RHN, founder of Nutriholist

"Maja's recipes are absolutely brilliant! I can't wait to try them all!"

—YUKIKO TANZI, founder of Foodie Yuki

bake it vegan

Simple, Delicious
Plant-Based Cakes, Cookies,
Brownies, Chocolates
and More

Maja Brekalo

Founder of Delicious & Healthy by Maya

PAGE STREET
PUBLISHING CO.

PAGE STREET
PUBLISHING CO.

Copyright © 2021 Maja Brekalo

First published in 2021 by

Page Street Publishing Co.

27 Congress Street, Suite 105

Salem, MA 01970

www.pagestreetpublishing.com

Distributed by Macmillan, sales in Canada by The Canadian Manda Group.

25 24 23 22 21 1 2 3 4 5

ISBN-13: 978-1-64567-239-5

ISBN-10: 1-64567-239-5

Library of Congress Control Number: 2020944071

Cover and book design by Meg Baskis for Page Street Publishing Co.

Photography by Maja Brekalo

Printed and bound in the United States

dedication

This book is dedicated to all the amazing people that follow
and support Delicious & Healthy by Maya. Without your
continuous love, I wouldn't have this job that I love so much,
and this book wouldn't have been possible.

contents

(GF = gluten-free recipe)

INTRODUCTION

Some of my favorite childhood memories involve baking with my mom. Although instead of baking, it was really me stealing and tasting the batter of whatever my mom was baking. Even today I love dipping my hands in flour, measuring ingredients, grinding nuts and mixing it all together. I started baking on my own at a pretty young age. I was about ten years old when I took my first baking steps. At the time, I only knew how to make conventional cakes and sweets, but I never ate them, as I could never digest those kinds of desserts. I didn't follow a vegan diet as a child, but I had a very sensitive stomach and conventional desserts made me sick. I struggled a lot with weak digestion, heartburn and nausea until I started following a pescatarian diet, and later I became a vegan.

You can imagine how my life was changed when I first discovered healthy vegan baking and vegan desserts. I could finally have cake! Since then, my fascination with vegan baking has never tired.

Coming up with healthier and vegan versions of conventional desserts has become my mission in recent years, as I realized that most people, including my family, find it so much harder to follow a vegan diet when it comes to making and eating cakes and sweets compared to savory foods. Vegan baking is also often more intimidating than vegan cooking because making traditional desserts work with unconventional ingredients is so much more difficult than "veganizing" savory favorites. And if you're trying to create those desserts using only wholesome, unprocessed ingredients, it becomes even more complicated.

My goal is to solve this problem by creating amazing, approachable vegan desserts that are good for you without sacrificing that feeling of indulgence. This cookbook is a collection of fuss-free, delicious, wholesome recipes that can be easily made by even the most inexperienced bakers.

I've also worked hard to develop plenty of gluten-free vegan recipes for this book. This is because gluten-free food, or at least conventionally grown wheat-free food, suits me so much better. I say conventional wheat-free food because I do use spelt flour in addition to gluten-free flours like rice and buckwheat. Spelt is considered to be a distant relative of wheat, but it hasn't been genetically modified and contains much less gluten compared to conventional wheat. I find it to be great in recipes that need a small amount of gluten, while still being a healthy and wholesome option.

I realize that many of you, like me, are out there searching for gluten-free baking recipes that actually work, so I've made it easier for you to find them in this book by marking them gluten-free, "GF," in the table of contents. I've also marked applicable recipes "grain free" and "nut free" throughout the manuscript, so vegan bakers with other dietary restrictions will also know which tasty options will work best for them. I hope these classifications will help you get the best use out of this book!

Here you'll find only nutritious "real-food" ingredients—you won't find any shortcuts, secretly processed vegan products or ingredients adding empty, unhealthy calories. I've also tried to incorporate as many highly nutritious ingredients as possible, like substituting wheat flour with higher-quality grains; swapping part of the flour with nuts or seeds; using healthy fats like extra virgin olive or coconut oil; and sneaking in veggies or beans for added protein, fiber, healthy fats and overall nutritional value. Vegan butter is the only refined ingredient included, but it will only be used in the smallest amounts; vegan butter can also be nutritious, as long as you make sure to use one that does not contain trans fats or any other highly processed ingredients.

These recipes are for everyone, whether you're vegan and craving your old favorite desserts, or you're just trying to eat healthier by switching to a plant-based diet. Even though some of these plant-based desserts won't taste exactly the same as their conventional, unhealthy, sugar- and fat-loaded counterparts, their flavors will still be out-of-this-world amazing—or even more so because you can feel confident that you're indulging in a dessert that not only tastes good, but serves your body well.

I'm so excited for you to try these recipes, especially since I've been getting so much positive feedback from my Delicious & Healthy by Maya blog and Instagram followers as well as from "real-life" friends. They don't say that these recipes taste really delicious "for a healthy dessert." They say, "These are sensational! Please open a pastry shop!"

Thank you for picking up this book and having faith in my recipes. Maybe you've been following my Delicious & Healthy by Maya blog or Instagram account, or maybe you just ran into this cookbook at the bookshop or online. Either way, I'd like you to know that I appreciate you, and I appreciate all the support I've been given over the years. Without your support, this cookbook would not have come to be.

My first book baby, *My Happy Food*—a vegan cookbook published in my home country of Croatia—quickly became a #1 bestselling cookbook and reached #4 on the overall bestsellers list. I was stoked that my predominantly non-vegan country had embraced my vegan cookbook. I'm so grateful for all the support, amazing reviews and hundreds of messages I've received from readers saying how much they enjoyed the simplicity and deliciousness of my recipes.

I hope *Bake It Vegan* will connect with and inspire readers in the same way. I also hope bringing these recipes into your life will give you that feeling of joy and indulgence that, for me, only healthy and delicious food can give.

Love,

Maya xx

VEGAN BAKING TIPS AND TRICKS

So many people find vegan baking intimidating and even scary. This is why I wanted to include a list of tips, tricks and swaps for vegan baking as well as for general dessert-making—including raw desserts. If you read this, I promise it will make baking and dessert-making so much easier and less scary, and it will help you get a perfect (or at least close-to-perfect) result every single time.

· Always use room-temperature ingredients unless stated otherwise (as in using chilled coconut oil in a galette crust or chilled coconut milk for whipping coconut cream).

· Sift all dry ingredients—this will make your baked goods fluffier and softer.

· Do not overmix the batter! This is so important! This might be my most important tip. Fold dry ingredients with wet ones until just combined; leaving a few flour pockets is fine. Overmixed batter means chewy and dense cake, pancakes, muffins and breads—it just spoils all of it.

· Before folding berries into your cake batter, coat them with some flour. This will prevent them from sinking to the bottom of the cake while baking.

· Don't let the prepared batter sit, unless otherwise noted. Put it into the oven immediately; letting it sit may result in a dense cake.

· Always preheat your oven for at least 15 to 20 minutes before you need it.

· Never open the oven during the first two-thirds of the baking time. This causes cakes to sink.

· Keep an eye on your goodies. Start checking a few minutes before the indicated time of baking has elapsed. All ovens are different, and baking times will vary slightly.

· Test if your baked goods are done by inserting a toothpick in the center. When you pull it out, it shouldn't have any wet batter on it. It should only have a few crumbs attached for baked cakes, or it can be slightly tinted with chocolate when you're making brownies.

· Unless indicated otherwise, you should always take the baked goods out of the pan as soon as possible and rest them on a cooling rack. If left inside of pans, they will continue baking, resulting in overcooked and dry treats.

· Always line the bottoms of your pans with parchment paper; it will prevent sticking and ease transferring your cakes. If you're using a rectangular or loaf pan, leave some of the paper hanging out of the sides to ease the removal of cakes.

· For muffins and cupcakes, I prefer using silicone liners. Paper liners can dry baked goods out. If you do use them, be sure to grease them to prevent sticking. I use coconut oil spray.

· Many of these recipes allow for vanilla powder or vanilla extract. Note that when using powder, the vanilla should be incorporated into the dry ingredients, and when using extract, the vanilla should be incorporated into the wet ingredients.

· I use oat milk in my recipes because it is neutral in flavor and rich in soluble fiber and good fats. But feel free to use almond milk instead, if that is what you prefer.

· One important note for all of you using metric measurements. You should always measure volume in milliliters in a measuring cup or with a spoon or teaspoon for smaller amounts (1 tbsp = 15 ml; 1 tsp = 5 ml). If you try to measure liquids in milliliters on a digital scale, you'll get an incorrect amount.

DECADENT CAKES

This chapter contains the essential dessert for every celebration. All the crowd-pleasers are present: luscious moist cakes that will impress your guests, delicious cupcakes to wow the little ones and holiday treats to be enjoyed by the whole family at special times.

These gorgeous cakes and cupcakes are my more wholesome and nourishing takes on the classics, which still taste so rich and indulgent that you'll fall in love with them. There is The Chocolate Cake (page 14), as I call it—a vegan version of our childhood favorite chocolate cake with chocolate frosting. The Strawberries and Cream Cake (page 23) is a light, dreamy summer dessert smothered in whipped coconut cream and fresh juicy strawberries. The Best Vegan Tiramisu (page 26) features layers of fluffy, rich chocolate cake infused with aromatic black coffee and luscious cashew cream, beautifully balanced with a dark intense cocoa layer. I couldn't ask for more!

Vegan baking can be challenging, and you might think that baking an amazing cake without using conventional ingredients like eggs, milk, butter and bleached wheat flour isn't possible. But let me prove you wrong. Nature gave us so many wholesome ingredients that can be used to make cakes that are just as good or even better than their traditional versions.

To make it easier for you guys, the list of ingredients I used in all these cake recipes is more or less the same in each one, with an odd ingredient thrown in here and there. After you've made your first shopping haul, you will be set; there will be no need to run to the store for every cake you decide to make because you'll probably have all the ingredients already stocked in your pantry. Make sure to pay close attention to my instructions and notes in these recipes, as they include important tips about how to make your vegan baking successful every time!

THE CHOCOLATE CAKE

I've been told many times that this cake is *the* chocolate cake. It has such an intense chocolate flavor while remaining wonderfully moist; it just melts in the mouth, and that creamy frosting . . . it is just perfect. I think it tastes exactly like the chocolate cakes of my childhood, or even better. I'm telling you, every single time I take the first bite, I feel like that six-year-old again. Make it for any celebration and your guests will adore you!

CAKE

2 cups (480 ml) oat milk, room temperature

2 tsp (10 ml) apple cider vinegar

2½ cups (310 g) white spelt flour

2 tbsp (20 g) tapioca starch

½ tsp fine Himalayan salt

1¼ cups (165 g) coconut sugar

1 tsp baking soda

2 tsp (7 g) baking powder

¼ tsp vanilla powder or ½ tsp vanilla extract

⅔ cup (60 g) unsweetened cocoa powder

1 tsp lemon juice

⅔ cup (160 ml) melted extra virgin coconut oil

VEGAN CHOCOLATE FROSTING

¼ cup (35 g) unrefined cocoa butter

1 cup (140 g) soaked cashews (see Note)

½ to ⅔ cup (120 to 160 ml) water

2 tbsp (25 g) chia seeds

6 small pitted dates (⅓ cup [50 g]), chopped

Pinch of fine Himalayan salt

1 tsp lemon juice

¼ cup (60 ml) maple or agave syrup

½ tsp vanilla powder or 1 tsp vanilla extract, optional

Pinch of cinnamon, optional

1 tsp rum, optional

4 to 5 tbsp (40 to 50 g) unsweetened cocoa powder

To make the chocolate cake, preheat the oven to 355°F (180°C) and grease and line the bottom of three 8-inch (20-cm) round springform pans with parchment paper.

Mix the milk with apple cider vinegar and leave it to sour for 10 to 15 minutes.

In a large bowl, sift the flour, tapioca starch, salt, sugar, baking soda, baking powder, vanilla and cocoa. In a small bowl, whisk together the lemon juice and melted coconut oil. Make a well in the dry ingredients, add the oil mixture and fold gently with a silicone spatula or a large wooden spoon. Pour in the soured milk and gently whisk until combined. The batter should be nice and smooth and not too thick.

Evenly divide the batter between the three prepared baking tins, and place them in the preheated oven. Bake for 15 minutes until the tops look firm and spring back when pressed. To check that they're done, insert a toothpick in the middle of each cake, piercing all the way through. If it comes out clean, the cakes are done; if there's any wet batter on the toothpick, continue baking for another 2 to 3 minutes and check again. Be careful not to overbake them; the cakes are thin and will dry out fast if left in the oven for too long.

Remove the cakes from the oven, allow them to cool slightly in the pan for 10 to 15 minutes, then carefully open the springforms and flip the cakes onto a wire rack to cool down completely and to flatten the domes a bit. The cakes will still have the domes once cooled, but you can level them by cutting off the top to get a neater cake, if you wish. The cakes should be cooled down completely before assembly.

To make the Vegan Chocolate Frosting, ensure all the ingredients are at room temperature. Melt the cocoa butter in a double boiler, place it with the cashews, water, chia seeds, dates, salt, lemon juice and syrup in a blender and blend until smooth. At this stage, you can also add optional ingredients like the vanilla, cinnamon or rum to add another interesting flavor to your frosting. You might have to stop and stir to help the process of blending. If necessary, you can also add a small amount of water, but be careful not to add too much to avoid runny frosting.

When the mixture is well blended, add the cocoa and blend until it incorporates into a smooth frosting. Transfer the mixture into a jar and refrigerate for at least 2 hours before use. It will firm up nicely. You can store it refrigerated for up to 1 week.

(continued)

CAKE ASSEMBLY
3 tbsp (45 ml) warm water

1 to 2 tsp (5 to 10 g) coconut sugar

1 tsp dark rum

TOPPINGS
Chocolate shavings, optional

Fresh berries, optional

To assemble the cake, mix the warm water with coconut sugar and rum until the sugar is dissolved. Allow the mixture to cool before assembly.

Take one cake and place it on a cake plate. Soak the cake with 1 tablespoon (15 ml) of the flavored water to add moisture, then frost with ½ cup (120 g) of the Vegan Chocolate Frosting. Top the first layer with the second cake and repeat the steps. Add the last layer, repeat the steps and frost the sides, reserving the last 2 to 3 tablespoons (30 to 45 g) of the frosting. Refrigerate the cake for a few hours. Take it out and frost the surface again so it is nice and neat. Return the cake to the refrigerator for another hour or so. You can also decorate the cake with some chocolate shavings or fresh berries.

To serve, take it out of the refrigerator 15 to 20 minutes before serving, so both the cake and frosting soften to reveal their best flavor and consistency.

Store the cake in a closed container refrigerated for up to 1 week.

NOTE: The cashews need to be soaked before use. This will make them softer and easier to blend, which will result in a super creamy consistency. Before starting the recipe, place the cashews in a medium-sized container, cover them with fresh water and leave them to soak for at least 3 hours.

APPLE MOLASSES CAKE

Incredibly soft and rich and just bursting with flavor, this cake is the bomb. The beautiful tenderness of the caramelized apples with the subtle aromas of spices and a hint of walnuts make it truly divine. Even the smallest slice of this cake will satisfy your senses. With a dollop of creamy Vegan Vanilla Frosting, it is my definition of pure heaven. I love eating this cake while it's still warm, but as it cools completely and rests for a few days, it will become even more delicious as the juice from the apples infuses the cake and all the flavors and spices become more pronounced.

CAKE

½ cup (120 ml) oat milk, room temperature

1 tsp apple cider vinegar

1 tbsp (15 g) golden flax seeds

3 tbsp (45 ml) water

½ cup (55 g) walnuts

½ cup (70 g) brown rice flour

½ cup (62 g) white spelt flour

½ tsp baking soda

½ tsp baking powder

3 pinches of fine Himalayan salt, divided

4 tbsp (40 g) coconut sugar, divided

1 tsp cinnamon, divided

1 tsp vanilla powder or 1 tsp vanilla extract

½ tsp lemon zest

1 tsp fresh ginger juice

1 tbsp (15 ml) lemon juice

¼ cup (60 ml) mild-tasting olive oil or melted extra virgin coconut oil

3 tbsp (45 ml) molasses

3 tbsp (30 g) coconut oil

2 cups (240 g) apples diced into ½-inch (1.3-cm) cubes

½ tsp vanilla extract

To make the cake, preheat the oven to 355°F (180°C). Grease the sides and bottom of an 8-inch (20-cm) round baking pan or a similarly-sized rectangular or square pan.

Mix the milk with the apple cider vinegar and leave it to sour for about 10 to 15 minutes. Grind the flax seeds and mix them with the water in a small bowl to make a flax egg. Set it aside to thicken. Finely grind the walnuts in a food processor. Set it aside.

In a large bowl, sift the flours, baking soda, baking powder, 2 pinches of salt, 1 tablespoon (10 g) of sugar, ½ teaspoon of cinnamon and vanilla. Mix in the lemon zest and ground walnuts. In a small bowl, whisk together the ginger juice, lemon juice, olive oil and molasses.

In a medium-sized pan, warm up the remaining 3 tablespoons (30 g) of the sugar and coconut oil. Whisk it and cook over a very low flame briefly, until the sugar is mostly melted into the oil. Toss in the apples with the remaining pinch of salt, remaining ½ teaspoon of cinnamon and vanilla. Fold to evenly cover the apples, and transfer them into the prepared baking pan using a silicone spatula. Distribute them evenly on the bottom.

Make a well in the dry ingredients and add the oil-molasses mixture and flax egg. Fold gently with a silicone spatula or a large wooden spoon. Pour in the soured milk and keep folding gently until just combined. Don't overmix it to avoid a chewy cake. Pour the batter carefully over the apples and shake the pan gently to level the top.

Bake it in your preheated oven for 30 to 35 minutes. The cake will be dark brown because of the molasses. The edges should be slightly more browned and the tops will have cracks when it is finished baking. Check if it is done by inserting a toothpick in the middle. It should come out clean, with just a few moist crumbs attached.

Remove the cake from the oven and allow it to cool completely in the pan.

(continued)

VEGAN VANILLA FROSTING

1 cup (140 g) soaked cashews (see Note on page 16)

¼ cup (60 ml) melted extra virgin coconut oil

¼ cup (60 ml) maple or agave syrup

1 tsp vanilla powder or 2 tsp (10 ml) vanilla extract

Pinch of fine Himalayan salt

2 tbsp (30 ml) lemon juice

⅓ to ½ cup (80 to 120 ml) water

¼ tsp cinnamon, optional

Lemon zest, optional

1 tsp rum, optional

You can serve as it is or with a dollop of Vegan Vanilla Frosting. To make the frosting, place all the ingredients except the cinnamon, lemon zest and rum in a blender and blend until smooth. Add more water to reach your desired consistency. You can add the cinnamon, lemon zest or rum for additional flavoring. Refrigerate the frosting for at least 1 hour before use. Serve the cake cut into slices with a dollop of the frosting on the side or on top of each slice.

Store the cake in a closed container at room temperature for up to 3 days or refrigerated for up to 1 week.

SACHER TORTE

This is one of the most intensely chocolate, indulgent treats I have ever tasted, and it is one of my favorite cakes in this chapter. Imagine a soft, rich cake with a melt-in-your-mouth consistency, united with tangy apricot jam and an intense dark chocolate glaze. I have yet to find a person who doesn't love it. Sacher Torte is a classic in Croatia, but it actually originated in Austria. It was created by a young chef named Franz Sacher for a prince in 19th-century Vienna. This beautiful-yet-simple cake is still one of the most famous Viennese culinary specialties, and my vegan-friendly version is equally, if not more, delicious! The Sacher Torte is at its best a day or two after assembling so the jam has time to soak into the cake. I recommend making it at least a day in advance.

CAKE

2 cups (480 ml) oat or almond milk, room temperature

2 tsp (10 ml) apple cider vinegar

2½ cups (310 g) white spelt flour

1 tbsp (10 g) tapioca starch

2 tsp (7 g) baking powder

1 tsp baking soda

1 tsp fine Himalayan salt

½ tsp vanilla powder or 1 tsp vanilla extract

⅔ cup (65 g) unsweetened cocoa powder

1½ cups (195 g) coconut sugar

⅔ cup (160 ml) melted extra virgin coconut oil

1 tsp lemon juice

1 cup (280 g) smooth apricot jam

Preheat the oven to 355°F (180°C).

Mix the milk with the vinegar and let it sit to sour for about 10 to 15 minutes.

Prepare two 8-inch (20-cm) round springform pans. Grease them lightly and cover the bottom with parchment paper.

Sift all the dry ingredients into a large bowl. In a smaller bowl, mix the oil and lemon juice and pour the mixture into the dry ingredients. Using a silicone spatula or a large wooden spoon, mix gently and add the soured milk gradually. You will get a fluffy, smooth batter.

Divide the batter equally between the two prepared springform pans. Shake them to level and tap gently a few times on the countertop so the bubbles are settled.

Put the pans in the oven, and bake the cakes for 25 minutes. After the time has elapsed, test if they're done with a toothpick. Insert it into the cakes, piercing it all the way to the bottom. If it comes out clean, with just a few crumbs on it, the cakes are done. If there's any batter on it, bake the cakes for another 5 minutes and test again. If the toothpick is still a little wet, leave it for another 5 minutes in the hot oven with the heat off.

Transfer the cake pans to a cooling rack and leave them to cool for about 10 minutes. When they're cool enough to be taken out of the pan, turn the cakes over on the cooling rack. Remove the paper. Leave the cakes to cool upside down so the tops flatten.

When the cakes are completely cooled down, place the jam in a small pot and warm it over a low flame, stirring until smooth. Turn the bottom cake upside down to get an even surface on top so the cakes will neatly stack. Alternatively, use a knife to cut the tops of the cakes to level them. Brush the top of both cake halves with the jam and place one on top of the other. Brush the sides and top with the jam as well.

(continued)

CHOCOLATE GLAZE

⅓ cup (50 g) unrefined cocoa butter

⅓ cup (80 ml) maple syrup

5 tbsp (50 g) unsweetened cocoa powder

3 tbsp (45 ml) oat milk

To prepare the glaze, melt the cocoa butter in a double boiler, then add the syrup and stir until combined. Add the cocoa and keep stirring until smooth. Remove it from the boiler and add the milk, whisking continuously until smooth.

Apply the glaze to the cake using a spatula. Glaze the sides and top of the cake, and smooth it out as best as you can. Place the cake in the refrigerator to firm up.

Remove the cake from the refrigerator at least half an hour before serving, so both the sponge and the glaze soften. If you're letting the cake rest for a day or more before serving, keep it in the refrigerator in an airtight container to avoid drying out the cake. It will keep for up to 10 days.

STRAWBERRIES *and* CREAM CAKE

NUT FREE | YIELD: 1 (9-INCH [23-CM]) CAKE; 12-14 SLICES

This is such a dreamy cake. Layers of soft cake, luscious coconut cream and juicy strawberries are guaranteed to take you to heaven with every delicious bite. I catch myself dreaming of it during winter months, impatiently waiting for strawberry season. It's super easy to make, with a cake you'll whip up in no time, cream that is basically coconut milk with a handful of ingredients and then strawberries. . . . So delicious and full of goodness.

CAKE

2 cups (480 ml) oat milk, room temperature

2 tsp (10 ml) apple cider vinegar

2½ cups (310 g) white spelt flour

2 tbsp (20 g) tapioca starch

2 tsp (7 g) baking powder

1 tsp baking soda

½ tsp fine Himalayan salt

½ tsp vanilla powder or 1 tsp vanilla extract

1¼ cups (165 g) coconut sugar

⅔ cup (160 ml) melted extra virgin coconut oil

½ tsp lemon juice

STRAWBERRIES

2 cups (270 g) fresh strawberries

1 tsp lemon juice

Maple syrup or a pinch of powdered stevia, to taste

Preheat the oven to 355°F (180°C).

Prepare two 9-inch (23-cm) round springform pans. Grease the sides and bottom lightly, and cover the bottoms with parchment paper.

To make the cake, mix the milk with the vinegar and let it sit to sour for 10 to 15 minutes.

Sift the flour with the tapioca starch, baking powder, baking soda, salt, vanilla and coconut sugar. In a smaller bowl, mix the coconut oil and lemon juice and add them to the dry ingredients. Using a silicone spatula or a whisk, mix gently while adding the soured milk gradually. The batter will be fluffy and smooth.

Pour half of the batter into each pan. Shake them to even the tops and tap gently on the countertop to release the air bubbles. Bake the cakes for 30 minutes. After the time has elapsed, test if they're done with a toothpick. Insert it in the cake, piercing it all the way to the bottom. If it comes out clean, with just a few crumbs on it, it is done. If there's any wet batter on it, bake it for another 2 to 3 minutes and test again. Leave them to cool down until they're cool enough to be taken out of the pan. Run a paring knife around the edges, and turn them over on the cooling rack. Remove the paper. Leave them upside down so the tops will flatten.

To prepare the strawberries, wash them and remove the stems. Slice thinly and season with lemon juice and maple syrup to taste, then refrigerate.

(continued)

COCONUT WHIPPED CREAM

1 (14-oz [400-ml]) can full-fat coconut milk or coconut cream, chilled for 1 to 3 days in advance (see Notes)

½ tsp vanilla extract

Pinch of stevia powder or 1 to 2 tsp (5 to 10 ml) maple syrup, optional

To prepare the Coconut Whipped Cream, chill a bowl and the beaters of your mixer for about a half hour in the refrigerator. The chilled full-fat coconut cream will separate from the water in the coconut milk or coconut cream. It will accumulate at the top and harden; be careful not to shake or tip the can to keep this separation of the cream and liquid. Open the can of coconut milk and scoop out only the hard coconut cream that settled on top. Place the coconut cream into the chilled bowl. Be sure not to include any water, but feel free to save the coconut water to use in smoothies—it is very nutritious!

Using a hand mixer, whip the cream for 30 seconds until creamy. Then add vanilla and stevia or maple syrup, if using, and mix until creamy and smooth, for about 1 minute or until fluffy. The whipped cream should be prepared just before serving.

Assemble the cake right before serving. Place one cake layer on a cake plate, frost it with coconut cream using cold or chilled utensils and top the cream with the prepared strawberries. Reserve a handful of strawberries for topping the cake. Add the second cake layer, frost it and top with the remaining strawberries.

Store any leftovers in the refrigerator in an airtight container for up to 3 days.

NOTES: Be sure to use a coconut milk brand that contains no other ingredients but coconut and water; some brands add emulsifiers that keep the milk from separating. The separation is crucial for the Coconut Whipped Cream.

You can make the cakes 1 to 2 days in advance. Wrap them in plastic wrap or keep in an airtight container and store in the refrigerator until needed.

THE BEST VEGAN TIRAMISU

I'm a huge coffee lover, and this combination of super chocolaty cake soaked in strong coffee and rum, topped with luscious and sweet vanilla cashew cream and generously dusted with a layer of pure cocoa—which perfectly complements the overall sweetness with its slight bitterness—is a touch of heaven. This is not a usual tiramisu recipe, but I was sold on the first bite. This recipe came to be by a total coincidence. I had some leftover cake bits from leveling a chocolate cake and instead of tossing them, I decided to try and make a tiramisu using unconventional ingredients. It turned out to be one of my absolute favorites in this book.

CAKE

¾ to 1 cup (180 to 240 ml) oat milk, room temperature

½ tsp apple cider vinegar

1¼ cups (160 g) white spelt flour

1 tbsp (10 g) tapioca starch

½ tsp baking soda

½ tsp baking powder

2 pinches of fine sea salt

½ cup (65 g) coconut sugar

½ tsp vanilla powder or 1 tsp vanilla extract

⅓ cup (35 g) unsweetened cocoa

⅓ cup (80 ml) melted extra virgin coconut oil

1 tsp lemon juice

CASHEW TIRAMISU FILLING

2 cups (280 g) soaked cashews (see Note on page 16)

½ cup (120 ml) melted extra virgin coconut oil

½ to ⅔ cup (120 to 160 ml) water

1 tbsp (15 ml) lemon juice

2 pinches of salt

1 tsp vanilla powder or 2 tsp (10 ml) vanilla extract

½ cup (120 ml) maple syrup

2 tbsp (30 ml) dark rum

To make the cake, preheat the oven to 350°F (175°C). Grease and line an 8-inch (20-cm) square baking pan.

Mix the milk with the apple cider vinegar and leave it to sour for 10 to 15 minutes.

In a large bowl, sift the flour, tapioca starch, baking soda, baking powder, salt, sugar, vanilla and cocoa. In a small bowl, mix the melted oil and lemon juice. Make a well in the dry ingredients, add the oil mixture and fold gently with a silicone spatula or a large wooden spoon. Pour in the soured milk gradually; using a whisk, whisk gently until just combined. The batter should quickly become smooth. Be careful to not overmix; it could make the end result chewy.

Pour the batter into the lined pan, and gently shake and tap the pan on the counter-top to release any air bubbles and to even the top. Bake it for 20 to 25 minutes, or until the center looks set and the inserted toothpick comes out clean and only slightly tinted with chocolate.

Transfer it to a cooling rack and let it cool for 10 to 15 minutes. Then take the cake out of the pan to cool down completely on the rack.

To make the filling, wash and drain the soaked cashews and place them in the blender with the rest of the ingredients. At first, add only ½ cup (120 ml) of water and blend. If needed, add more and keep blending until you get a perfectly smooth texture.

To assemble the tiramisu, return the cake to the same dish or a slightly bigger one (about 9 inches [23 cm] in size) and cut it length-wise in 1-inch (2.5-cm) pieces. If you are using a bigger dish, separate the pieces evenly. This way, you get pieces similar in size to lady fingers, which are normally used in a conventional tiramisu.

(continued)

COFFEE

1 cup (240 ml) cold strong coffee

3 tbsp (45 ml) dark rum

2 tbsp (20 g) unsweetened cocoa powder, or to taste, for sifting

Place the cold coffee in a measuring cup, add the rum and stir. Pour the prepared coffee mixture over the cake and let it soak in for a few minutes. Pour the cashew filling over the soaked cake and shake the pan to level the filling.

Sift the cocoa, evenly and generously, in a thick layer on the top. Transfer it into the refrigerator and let it set for at least 3 to 4 hours before serving.

You can sift even more cocoa over it before serving and slicing it, as it can soak in and become slightly wet. I like having a lot of cocoa powder on top as its bitterness balances nicely with the sweetness of the filling and cake.

Keep the cake covered with a lid or cover the dish with plastic wrap. You can refrigerate it for up to 10 days in the refrigerator. It can also be frozen for up to 3 months. Let it defrost at room temperature or in the refrigerator and sift with more cocoa before serving.

To serve, you can scoop the tiramisu and serve it in a glass jar. You can also add more cold coffee and sift more cocoa over it, if you like the flavors. Or, you can cut the cake in slices using a sharp knife, and serve it on the plates sifted with more cocoa.

BLACK FOREST MIXED BERRY CAKE

YIELD: 1 (10-INCH [25-CM]) CAKE; 16 SLICES

This is my take on classic Black Forest cake—a rich chocolate cake with cherry compote and buttercream. Traditionally, it is made with loads of butter and sugar, which is a big no for me. Since I've always loved this combination of flavors, I set my mind to make a lighter version that will not compromise the taste. I created this super chocolaty and rich vegan cake with a berry sauce made from scratch and a cashew cream frosting; it came together perfectly!

CAKE

1 tbsp (15 g) flax seeds

3 tbsp (45 ml) water

2⅔ cups (640 ml) oat or almond milk, room temperature

2½ tsp (13 ml) apple cider vinegar

3½ cups (450 g) white spelt flour

3 tbsp (30 g) tapioca starch

3 tsp (10 g) baking powder

1½ tsp (10 g) baking soda

1 tsp fine Himalayan salt

1 tsp vanilla powder or 2 tsp (10 ml) vanilla extract

1 cup (100 g) unsweetened cocoa powder

2 cups (260 g) coconut sugar

1 cup (240 ml) melted extra virgin coconut oil

1 tsp lemon juice

BERRY SAUCE

2 cups (300 g) frozen or fresh mixed berries

2 tbsp (30 ml) maple syrup

1 tsp tapioca starch

2 tsp (10 ml) water

To make the cake, preheat the oven to 350°F (175°C). Prepare two 10-inch (25-cm) round springform pans. Grease them lightly and cover the bottom with parchment paper.

Prepare the flax egg by grinding the flax seeds using a coffee bean grinder or a small food processor, mix them with the water and leave to thicken.

Mix the milk with the vinegar and let it sit to sour for 10 to 15 minutes.

Sift the flour with the tapioca starch, baking powder, baking soda, salt, vanilla, cocoa and sugar. In a smaller bowl, mix the oil and lemon juice and add it to the dry ingredients. Add the prepared flax egg and, using a spatula, mix the batter gently while adding the soured milk gradually. You will get a nice fluffy batter that is smooth and not thick.

Pour half of the batter into each pan. Shake them to even and smooth out the top. Tap them gently on the countertop to release any trapped air bubbles.

Bake the cakes for 25 to 30 minutes. After 25 minutes, test if they're done with a toothpick. Insert it in the cake, piercing it all the way to the bottom. If it comes out clean, with just a few crumbs on it, it is done. If there's any wet batter on it, bake it for another 5 minutes and test again. Take them out of the oven and place onto the cooling rack and leave to cool for 15 to 20 minutes. When they're cool enough to be taken out of the pans, run a paring knife around the edges, and turn them over on the cooling rack. Remove the paper and leave them upside down so the tops will flatten.

To prepare the berry sauce, place the berries in a pan, season them with the syrup, cover and cook over a low flame for about 15 minutes, until the berries are nice and soft. They should be coming apart when stirred. In a small bowl, dilute the tapioca starch with the water and pour it into the berries while continuously stirring. The sauce should thicken. Turn it off and taste the sauce for your desired sweetness; add more syrup if needed and leave it to cool while you prepare the cream frosting.

(continued)

WHITE CHOCOLATE CREAM FROSTING

½ cup (70 g) unrefined cocoa butter

2 cups (280 g) soaked cashews (see Note on page 16)

½ to ⅔ cup (120 to 160 ml) oat milk, room temperature

2 tbsp (30 ml) lemon juice

2 pinches of salt

2 tsp (10 g) vanilla powder

½ cup (120 ml) agave syrup

1 cup (130 g) fresh berries, optional

To make the frosting, melt the cocoa butter in a double boiler and set it aside.

Wash and drain the soaked cashews, place them in the blender, add the rest of the ingredients and the melted cocoa butter and blend. To start, only use ½ cup (120 ml) of milk and add more if needed to blend it into a smooth cream. Pour the cream frosting in a jar and store in the refrigerator for at least 2 to 3 hours to chill and firm up a bit.

When the cakes are completely cooled down, you can assemble the cake. It is important to leave them to cool before frosting so they will firm up and not melt the frosting.

To assemble the cake, place one cake on a cake plate upside down; the bottom will be more leveled. Spread half of the berry sauce on top and then one-third of the cream frosting. Place the second cake on top of it, bottom side down. Spread the rest of the sauce on it, and then frost the whole cake with the rest of the cream frosting. You can decorate it with fresh berries of your choice, if using. Refrigerate for at least an hour to set.

To serve, let it warm up just a little bit at room temperature so the cake softens to reach its best flavor and consistency. Store the cake in a sealed container in the refrigerator for up to 1 week.

NOTE: I prefer making everything a day in advance and assembling the cake the next day. You can make the cakes 1 or 2 days in advance for convenience, but also because they will become softer and more moist in the days after baking. Wrap them in plastic wrap or store them in an airtight container to prevent them from drying out, and place them in the refrigerator until needed.

RASPBERRY WHITE CHOCOLATE COFFEE CAKE

GLUTEN FREE | YIELD: 16 BARS

This lovely cake is quite a flavor explosion. The sweetness of white chocolate and vanilla, the intense nuttiness of roasted hazelnuts and the tanginess of raspberries and lemon all combine in a beautiful harmony that will satisfy all your sweet cravings. The only problem might be stopping yourself from eating it all in just one sitting.

2 tbsp (30 g) golden flax seeds

6 tbsp (90 ml) water

⅔ cup plus 2 tbsp (190 ml) oat or almond milk, room temperature

1 tsp apple cider vinegar

1½ cups (240 g) cooked or canned white beans

⅔ cup (160 ml) maple or agave syrup

⅓ tsp Himalayan salt

1 tsp vanilla powder or 2 tsp (10 ml) vanilla extract

¼ cup (60 ml) mild-tasting olive oil

3 tsp (15 ml) lemon juice

½ cup (75 g) roasted hazelnuts

⅔ cup plus ½ tbsp (115 g) brown rice flour, divided

⅓ cup (50 g) buckwheat flour

½ tsp xanthan gum

1 tsp baking powder

1 tsp baking soda

1 cup (130 g) raspberries, divided

½ cup (90 g) chopped vegan white chocolate or vegan white chocolate chips, divided

Preheat the oven to 350°F (175°C). Arrange a rack in the bottom third of the oven. Grease the bottom and sides of an 8-inch (20-cm) square pan and line it with parchment paper, letting the excess hang over the sides.

Prepare the flax egg by grinding the flax seeds using a coffee bean grinder or a small food processor; mix them with the water and leave it to thicken. Next, mix the milk with the apple cider vinegar and leave it to sour for 10 to 15 minutes.

Wash, drain and pat the beans dry to avoid a bean flavor. Put them in a food processor with the syrup, salt, vanilla, oil and lemon juice. Blend until smooth and creamy.

Grind the hazelnuts in a food processor and place them in a bowl; sift in ⅔ cup (110 g) of the brown rice flour, buckwheat flour, xanthan gum, baking powder and baking soda. Mix to distribute evenly.

Add the mixture of blended beans to the dry ingredients and fold gently with a silicone spatula or a large spoon. Next, add the prepared flax egg. Keep mixing and add the soured milk gradually. Gently fold until the ingredients are just barely combined; don't overmix. It's okay if you can see a few traces of flour. The consistency should be fairly thick but still pourable.

Sift the remaining ½ tablespoon (5 g) of brown rice flour onto two-thirds of the raspberries and coat them gently. Gently fold the raspberries and white chocolate into the batter, reserving about 5 to 6 pieces of chocolate. Pour the prepared batter into the lined pan. Shake it gently to level the top and arrange the reserved raspberries and chocolate. Press them gently into the batter.

Bake the cake for 35 to 40 minutes. After 35 minutes, if the top looks slightly browned on the edges and there are some cracks, test if the cake is fully baked by piercing the center with a toothpick. It should come out clean, or with a few crumbs attached. If there's any wet batter left, bake for another 5 minutes and test again. When the cake is done, the top will be golden brown and the cake will detach slightly from the raspberries.

Transfer the pan to a wire rack to cool for 15 to 20 minutes. Remove the cake and transfer to a rack to cool down completely. Slice it into 2-inch (5-cm) squares.

Refrigerate the cake in a sealed container for up to 1 week. Take it out of the refrigerator before serving, and leave it on a countertop for 10 to 15 minutes to soften before eating. You can also freeze it for up to 3 months.

STRAWBERRY LEMON SPONGE CAKE

NUT FREE | YIELD: 1 (10-INCH [25-CM]) ROUND CAKE; 14-16 SLICES

A beautifully moist cake filled with juicy, fragrant strawberries spells summer on the plate. This rich-tasting cake is easy to whip up, while the zing of the lemon beautifully complements and brings out the sweetness and aroma of strawberries. To make it more festive, frost the top with Vegan Vanilla Frosting (page 19) or Coconut Whipped Cream (page 25).

1 cup (240 ml) oat milk, room temperature

2 tsp (10 ml) apple cider vinegar

2 tbsp (30 g) golden flax seeds

6 tbsp (90 ml) water

2½ cups (310 g) white spelt flour, plus extra to coat the strawberries

½ tsp salt

½ tsp vanilla powder or 1 tsp vanilla extract

1 tsp baking powder

1 tsp baking soda

Zest of one unwaxed lemon (about 1 tsp of zest; see Notes)

⅓ cup (80 ml) melted extra virgin coconut oil

½ cup (120 ml) agave or maple syrup

4 tbsp (60 ml) lemon juice

2 cups (270 g) strawberries, halved or quartered depending on the size, divided

Vegan Vanilla Frosting (page 19), optional

Fresh strawberries, optional

Preheat the oven to 355°F (180°C) and prepare a 10-inch (25-cm) round spring-form pan by greasing the bottom and sides and lining the bottom with parchment paper.

Mix the milk with the apple cider vinegar and set it aside to sour for 10 to 15 minutes. To make the flax egg, grind the flax seeds in a coffee bean grinder or a small food processor and mix with the water in a small bowl. Leave it to thicken.

Sift the flour with the salt, vanilla, baking powder and baking soda into a large mixing bowl. Add the lemon zest and mix to evenly distribute the ingredients.

Place the oil, syrup and lemon juice into a small bowl and whisk. Add the flax egg and the wet mixture to the flour mixture. Gently fold the batter with a silicone spatula or a large wooden spoon. Gradually pour in the soured milk and keep folding gently until just combined. The batter should be lumpy and not smooth. Do not overmix. Coat two-thirds of the strawberries with some flour and gently fold them into the batter; reserve one-third of the strawberries for the topping. Transfer the batter into the prepared baking pan, smooth the surface with a spatula and arrange the strawberries on top. Press them in gently so they are partially sunk into the batter.

Bake the cake in the preheated oven for 35 to 40 minutes. Check if it is done after 35 minutes, if the top is nicely browned and slightly cracked, and the cake is separating from the strawberry pieces, pierce the center all the way through with a toothpick. If it comes out clean, with just a few crumbs attached, it is done. If there's any wet batter, keep baking for another 5 minutes and test again.

When done, take the cake out of the oven and place the pan on a cooling rack; leave the cake to cool in the pan.

Serve it as is or with a dollop of Vegan Vanilla Frosting and fresh strawberries, if using. Store the cake in a sealed container or wrapped tightly on a countertop for up to 3 days. Store it in a sealed container in the refrigerator for up to 7 days or freeze for up to 1 month.

NOTES: This cake becomes even more delicious and fragrant as it sits, allowing the moisture from the fruits to be released into the cake and the flavors of the strawberries and lemon to become more pronounced. If possible, I recommend making it 1 day in advance.

Always use unwaxed organic lemons if using the rind.

THE MOST INDULGENT LAMINGTONS

These soft little cakes are one of my favorite childhood desserts—my grandmother used to make them for Christmas. Biting into one of these intense dark chocolate coconutty cakes still brings back the fondest of memories. This is my version of the classic lamingtons—they are a little more wholesome, but just as delicious.

CAKE

½ cup (120 ml) oat milk, room temperature

1 tsp apple cider vinegar

½ cup (70 g) brown rice flour

½ cup (62 g) white spelt flour

1 tbsp (10 g) tapioca starch

2 pinches of fine Himalayan salt

½ tbsp (5 g) baking powder

½ tsp baking soda

¼ tsp vanilla powder or ½ tsp vanilla extract

½ cup (60 g) almond or hazelnut meal

1 tsp lemon juice

¼ cup (60 ml) melted extra virgin coconut oil

¼ cup (60 ml) maple syrup

CHOCOLATE

⅓ cup (80 ml) melted extra virgin coconut oil

6 tbsp (90 ml) maple syrup

1 cup (100 g) unsweetened cocoa powder

⅔ cup (180 ml) oat milk

2 tsp (10 ml) dark rum, optional

2 cups (150 g) shredded coconut, as needed

To make the cake, preheat the oven to 350°F (175°C) and prepare an 8-inch (20-cm) square baking pan by greasing the bottom and sides and lining the bottom with parchment paper.

Mix the milk with the apple cider vinegar and leave it to sour for 10 to 15 minutes.

In a large bowl, sift the flours, tapioca starch, salt, baking powder, baking soda and vanilla. Add the almond meal into the dry ingredients and mix, using a whisk to combine. In a small bowl, whisk the lemon juice, oil and maple syrup. Next, make a well in the dry ingredients, add the wet mixture and fold gently with a silicone spatula or a large wooden spoon. Gently pour in the soured milk and whisk until combined. The batter should be smooth and not too thick.

Pour the batter into the prepared baking pan and bake for 15 to 20 minutes until the top looks firm and springs back when pressed. It should also be lightly golden around the edges. To check, insert a toothpick in the middle, piercing all the way through. If it comes out clean, the cake is done. If there's any wet batter on it, continue baking for another 3 to 5 minutes and test again. Be careful not to overbake; the cake is thin and will dry out if baked too long.

Remove the cake from the oven and allow it to slightly cool in the pan, then remove it from the pan and transfer it to a wire rack to cool down completely.

To prepare the chocolate, add oil and maple syrup to a medium-sized bowl and whisk to combine, add the cocoa and keep whisking till smooth. Gradually add the milk, 1 tablespoon (15 ml) at a time, until you have smooth chocolate. If the chocolate is too thick, it will tear off pieces of the cake when dipped in, so add more milk if necessary. If using, add the rum to the chocolate.

Place the coconut in a shallow bowl or a deep plate. Cut the cake into 1½-inch (4-cm) cubes. You should have 36 to 42 pieces.

Using two forks, gently dip the cakes in the chocolate until they are completely covered and transfer them to the bowl with the coconut. Be careful not to leave the cake cubes in the chocolate for too long, or they will fall apart. Gently roll the chocolate-covered cubes in coconut shreds until coated, and place them on parchment paper. Refrigerate them for at least an hour to set.

Keep the lamingtons refrigerated in a closed container for up to 10 days. Take them out of the refrigerator 15 to 20 minutes before serving to soften.

EASY RASPBERRY CAKE

YIELD: 1 (8-INCH [20-CM]) CAKE; 10–12 SLICES

This juicy rich cake has fresh raspberries baked into it, making it a light, refreshing treat. Imagine biting into a soft, delicious cake and hitting the juicy tart raspberries confined inside . . . so good! Add a dollop of Vegan Vanilla Frosting (page 19) and more fresh raspberries on top, and it becomes a flavor bomb!

2 tbsp (30 g) golden flax seeds

6 tbsp (90 ml) water

1 cup (240 ml) oat milk, room temperature

1 tsp apple cider vinegar

1 cup (140 g) brown rice flour

1 cup (125 g) white spelt flour, plus extra to coat the berries

1 tsp baking soda

1 tsp baking powder

⅓ tsp fine Himalayan salt

1 tsp vanilla powder or 2 tsp (10 ml) vanilla extract

2 tbsp (20 g) coconut sugar

1 tbsp (12 g) chia seeds

½ cup (70 g) almonds

½ cup (120 ml) maple or agave syrup

½ cup (120 ml) melted extra virgin coconut oil

1 tbsp (15 ml) lemon juice

1 small apple

1 cup (140 g) raspberries, plus more for topping, optional

Vegan Vanilla Frosting (page 19), optional

Preheat the oven to 355°F (180°C) and prepare an 8-inch (20-cm) round spring-form pan. Grease the bottom and sides with some coconut oil and line the bottom with parchment paper.

Grind the flax seeds in a coffee bean grinder or a small food processor, and mix them with the water in a small bowl to make the flax egg. Leave it aside to thicken.

Mix the milk with the apple cider vinegar and leave it to sour for 10 to 15 minutes.

Sift the flours with the baking soda, baking powder, salt, vanilla powder and sugar into a large mixing bowl. Add the chia seeds. Place the almonds in a food processor, and grind them to a fine meal, then add them to the dry ingredients. Whisk the mixture to combine.

In a small bowl, place the syrup, oil and lemon juice. Whisk to combine.

Peel and grate the apple. Make a well in the dry ingredients, and add the oil mixture and the flax egg. Fold gently with a silicone spatula or a large wooden spoon. Next, gradually pour in the soured milk and keep folding gently until just combined. Add in the grated apple and keep folding. Do not overmix; a few pockets of flour left in the batter is fine. Sift the spelt flour over the raspberries with some spelt flour and toss to cover. Fold them gently into the batter.

Transfer the batter into the prepared baking pan, shake it gently to level and smooth the surface with a spatula if needed.

Bake the cake for 40 minutes. Check if it is done after 35 minutes, piercing the center all the way through with a toothpick. If it comes out almost clean, with just a few crumbs attached to it, it is done. If it's covered in wet batter, keep baking for another 5 minutes and check again. If there's still just a bit of wet batter attached to the toothpick, bake for another 2 to 3 minutes and check again.

Take the cake out of the oven, place it onto a cooling rack and leave it to cool down completely before slicing.

Serve it as it is or with more fresh raspberries, if using. For a luscious party version, frost the top or serve it with a dollop of Vegan Vanilla Frosting, if using.

Store the cake in a sealed container or wrapped tightly at room temperature for up to 3 days or for up to 7 days refrigerated.

PEAR AND GINGER UPSIDE-DOWN CAKE

NUT FREE | YIELD: 1 (10-INCH [25-CM]) CAKE; 14-16 SLICES

When I was a kid, my mum's apple upside-down cake was my favorite dessert. Even now, I love this kind of simple, no-fuss cake that is soft, moist and fragrant and that just gets better in the days after baking. This is my take on the classic, but since I prefer pears to apples, it had to be a pear upside-down cake. I also added more varied, grown-up flavors like ginger, cinnamon, lemon and vanilla. I recommend leaving the cake to stand at room temperature for at least 1 day before eating it.

1 cup (240 ml) oat or almond milk, room temperature

1 tsp apple cider vinegar

2 tbsp (30 g) golden flax seeds

6 tbsp (90 ml) water

2 cups (250 g) white spelt flour

1 tsp baking powder

1 tsp baking soda

⅓ tsp Himalayan salt

½ tsp vanilla powder

½ tsp plus a dash of cinnamon, divided

½ cup (120 ml) extra virgin olive oil or melted extra virgin coconut oil

½ cup (120 ml) plus 2 tbsp (30 ml) maple syrup, plus more for brushing the cake, optional, divided

2 tbsp (30 ml) plus 1 tsp lemon juice, divided

1 to 2 tbsp (15 to 30 ml) fresh ginger juice (or 1 tsp ginger powder; see Note)

2 pears

Small pinch of salt

NOTE: To get the ginger juice, grate fresh ginger and squeeze it over a glass to collect the juice. You can use ginger powder, but I recommend the juice because it has a more subtle fruity flavor. You can make an apple upside-down cake using this same recipe.

Preheat the oven to 350°F (175°C) and prepare a 10-inch (25-cm) round baking pan. I recommend using a springform pan to remove the cake more easily. Grease the bottom and sides lightly, and cover the bottom with parchment paper.

Mix the milk with the apple cider vinegar and let it sit for at least 10 minutes while you prepare the rest of the ingredients. Grind the flax seeds using a coffee bean grinder or a small food processor, and mix them with the water for the flax egg. Sift the flour, baking powder, baking soda, Himalayan salt, vanilla and ½ teaspoon of the cinnamon into a large bowl. In a smaller bowl, whisk the oil, ½ cup (120 ml) of the syrup, 2 tablespoons (30 ml) of the lemon juice and ginger juice.

Make a well in the dry ingredients. Whisk the flax egg with the oil mixture and add it to the dry ingredients. Using a spatula, gently mix the ingredients while gradually adding the soured milk to get a smooth, fluffy batter. Be careful not to overmix; a few lumps of flour left is fine.

Peal the pears and cut them into ⅛-inch (3-mm)-thick slices. Season the pears with 2 tablespoons (30 ml) of the syrup, 1 teaspoon of the lemon juice, a dash of cinnamon and a pinch of salt. Place them in the baking pan, arranging the slices to cover the bottom of the pan, then carefully pour the batter on top. Shake the baking pan and tap it a few times on the countertop to settle any bubbles.

Bake the cake for 35 minutes. After the time has elapsed, test if the cake is done with a toothpick. Insert it in the cake, piercing it all the way to the bottom. If it comes out clean, with just a few crumbs on it, it is done. If there's any batter on it, bake it for another 5 minutes and test again.

Leave the cake to cool completely before taking it out of the pan. Turn it over onto a cake plate and remove the parchment paper.

You can brush the top of the cake with more maple syrup, if desired. Store the cake in a closed container at room temperature for up to 3 days. You can also store it in the refrigerator in a closed container for up to 1 week. I recommend leaving the cake to stand at room temperature for at least 1 day before eating it; it will become softer, more fragrant and more moist as the juice from the pears soaks into the cake.

CHERRY SHEET COFFEE CAKE

YIELD: 1 (15 X 10-INCH [38 X 25-CM]) CAKE; 20 SQUARES

This is a beautifully moist soft cake filled with juicy cherries and topped with crunchy almond flakes.
It would make a wonderful addition to your coffee or tea break, or even a sweet decadent breakfast.
For even more deliciousness, slather it with vanilla or chocolate frosting, top with more
fresh cherries and serve it as a rich celebration dessert.

2 cups (350 g) pitted cherries

4 tbsp (60 ml) maple syrup, divided

2 tbsp (30 g) golden flax seeds

6 tbsp (90 ml) water

1½ cups (360 ml) oat milk, room temperature

1 tsp apple cider vinegar

1½ cups (200 g) white spelt flour

1 tsp baking soda

1 tsp baking powder

⅔ tsp salt

1 tsp vanilla powder or 2 tsp (10 ml) vanilla extract

¼ tsp ground ginger

½ tsp cinnamon

½ cup (65 g) coconut sugar

1 tsp lemon zest (about 1 large unwaxed lemon)

3 tbsp (45 ml) lemon juice

½ cup (120 ml) mild-tasting olive oil or melted extra virgin coconut oil

2 tbsp (15 g) slivered flaked almonds

NOTE: You can frost this cake with Vegan Vanilla Frosting (page 19) or Vegan Chocolate Frosting (page 14) and top it with more fresh cherries.

Place the cherries in a bowl, season them with 1 tablespoon (15 ml) of maple syrup and set them aside.

Preheat the oven to 350°F (175°C) and prepare a 15 x 10-inch (38 x 25-cm) sheet pan by greasing it with coconut oil and lining the bottom with parchment paper.

To make the flax egg, grind the flax seeds in a coffee bean grinder or a small food processor and mix them with the water in a small bowl. Leave it to thicken for 10 to 20 minutes.

In a small bowl, mix the milk with the apple cider vinegar and leave it to sour for at least 10 minutes while you get all the other ingredients ready.

Sift the flour with the baking soda, baking powder, salt, vanilla, ginger, cinnamon and sugar into a large mixing bowl. Add the lemon zest.

Add the lemon juice, remaining 3 tablespoons (45 ml) of maple syrup and oil into a small bowl and whisk to combine. Add the oil mixture and flax egg to the dry ingredients and fold gently with a silicone spatula or a large wooden spoon. Pour in the soured milk and keep folding gently until just combined. Do not overmix; the batter can look a bit lumpy.

Transfer the batter into the prepared baking pan, smooth the surface with a spatula and scatter the cherries on top. Press them gently into the batter and sprinkle with slivered flaked almonds.

Bake the cake for 30 minutes on a middle rack until the top is nicely browned and cracked, and the cake starts to separate from the edges and the cherries. Test the cake by piercing the center all the way through with a toothpick. If it comes out clean, with just a few crumbs attached, it is done. If there is any wet batter on it, keep baking for another 5 minutes and test again.

Transfer it to the wire rack to cool completely in the pan. You can serve the cake while it's still warm. It will soften and become more moist and even more delicious in the next few days.

Store the cake in a sealed container or wrapped tightly on a countertop for up to 3 days. It can also be stored in the refrigerator for up to 7 days or in the freezer for up to 1 month.

THE FLUFFIEST CARROT CAKE CUPCAKES

YIELD: 12 CUPCAKES

Incredibly fluffy, soft and rich, just bursting with flavors of roasted hazelnuts, vanilla and lemon zest, these cupcakes are like little bites of paradise that will impress everyone. I have never had anyone describe these as anything less than amazing! The creamy frosting makes them even more indulgent, but trust me—even just as they are, preferably still warm out of the oven, they're incredibly decadent and healthy little treats.

1 cup (240 ml) oat milk, room temperature

1 tsp apple cider vinegar

1 tbsp (15 g) golden flax seeds

3 tbsp (45 ml) water

2 medium carrots

¼ cup (35 g) roasted hazelnuts

½ cup (70 g) brown rice flour

½ cup (65 g) white spelt flour

½ tsp baking soda

¼ tsp fine sea salt

½ cup (65 g) coconut sugar

Pinch of ginger powder

½ tsp vanilla powder or 1 tsp vanilla extract

1 tbsp (6 g) lemon zest

⅓ cup (80 ml) melted extra virgin coconut oil

2 tbsp (30 ml) lemon juice

OPTIONAL

Vegan Vanilla Frosting (page 19)

Coconut Whipped Cream (page 25)

Preheat the oven to 355°F (180°C). Line a 12-cup muffin pan with silicone or paper liners. If using paper liners, grease them with some coconut oil to prevent sticking.

Mix the milk with the apple cider vinegar and leave it to sour for 10 to 15 minutes. To make the flax egg, grind the flax seeds using a coffee bean grinder or a small food processor, and mix the ground seeds with the water in a small bowl. Set it aside for it to thicken.

Grate the carrots, squeeze out the juice from the gratings, measure ⅔ cup (90 g) of tightly packed carrot and set it aside. Grind the hazelnuts; it should result in about ⅓ cup (35 g) of hazelnut meal.

In a large bowl, sift the flours, baking soda, salt, sugar, ginger and vanilla. Mix in the hazelnut meal and lemon zest. In a small bowl, mix the oil and lemon juice. Make a well in the dry ingredients, add the oil mixture and flax egg and fold gently with a silicone spatula or a large wooden spoon. Next, pour in the soured milk and grated carrot and keep folding gently until just combined. The batter will be pretty thin and mostly smooth with some grated carrot and ground hazelnuts visible. Don't overmix.

Evenly divide the batter into the muffin cups. Each muffin cup should be two-thirds full.

Bake the cupcakes in the preheated oven for about 15 minutes until golden on top. They might look very soft but check by inserting a toothpick in the middle. If it comes out clean, with just a few moist crumbs attached, they're done.

Remove them from the oven and allow to slightly cool in the pan, then transfer the cupcakes to a wire rack. Let them cool for at least 20 minutes. You can have them as they are or decorated with Vegan Vanilla Frosting or Coconut Whipped Cream, if using.

Store the cupcakes unfrosted in a closed container at room temperature for up to 3 days or refrigerated for up to 1 week and frost before serving.

NOTE: The batter for these cupcakes is thinner than usual. This consistency makes the cupcakes softer than usual. However, if the batter looks way too thin, you can add 1 to 2 tablespoons (15 to 30 g) of brown rice flour to thicken it.

DARK CHOCOLATE CUPCAKES

NUT FREE | YIELD: 12 CUPCAKES

Super chocolaty and indulgent, these little bombs of flavor are so soft and moist. In combination with Chocolate Sweet Potato Frosting (page 77) or Vegan Chocolate Frosting (page 14), they are a true treat any of your guests will love.

1 cup (240 ml) oat milk, room temperature

1 tsp apple cider vinegar

1 tbsp (15 g) golden flax seeds

3 tbsp (45 ml) water

1 large apple

1¼ cups (160 g) white spelt flour

1 tbsp (10 g) tapioca starch

½ tsp baking soda

½ tsp baking powder

⅓ tsp fine sea salt

½ cup (65 g) coconut sugar

½ tsp vanilla powder or 1 tsp vanilla extract

⅓ cup (35 g) unsweetened cocoa powder

⅓ cup (80 ml) melted extra virgin coconut oil

1 tsp lemon juice

OPTIONAL

Chocolate Sweet Potato Frosting (page 77)

Vegan Chocolate Frosting (page 19)

Preheat the oven to 355°F (180°C). Line a 12-cup muffin pan with silicone or paper liners. If using paper liners, grease them with some coconut oil to prevent sticking.

Mix the milk with the apple cider vinegar and leave it to sour for 10 to 15 minutes. Grind the flax seeds in a coffee bean grinder or a small food processor, and mix with the water in a small bowl for a flax egg. Set aside for it to thicken. Peel and grate the apple and set it aside.

In a large bowl, sift the flour, tapioca starch, baking soda, baking powder, salt, sugar, vanilla and cocoa. In a small bowl, whisk together the oil and lemon juice. Next, make a well in the dry ingredients, and add in the oil mixture and flax egg. Fold gently with a silicone spatula or a large wooden spoon. Then pour in the soured milk and keep folding gently until combined. The batter should quickly become smooth. It will be runnier and smoother than muffin batter. Do not overmix.

Evenly divide the batter into the cups. Each cup should be two-thirds full.

Bake the cupcakes in the preheated oven for about 15 minutes until the top sets and an inserted toothpick comes out clean.

Remove the cupcakes from the oven and allow them to slightly cool in the pan, then transfer them to a wire rack. Let them cool for at least 20 minutes. You can eat them as they are or topped with Chocolate Sweet Potato Frosting or Vegan Chocolate Frosting, if using.

Be sure to let the cupcakes cool down completely before frosting. Store them, unfrosted, in a closed container at room temperature for up to 3 days or for up to 1 week in the refrigerator.

COOKIE HEAVEN

Everybody loves a good cookie, and these are all good, wholesome and delicious. You can eat them as a quick nutritious snack or an indulgent dessert to satisfy your sweet cravings. These delicious bites aren't loaded with unhealthy fats and sugar or made with plain flour, but they taste just as delicious as if they were! I use alternative flours made from almonds, coconut and whole grains like brown rice and spelt that not only make these cookies better for you but also give them beautiful aromas and consistencies that plain flour just doesn't have.

I have included some of my traditional Christmas favorites like rich, nutty gluten-free Buttery Almond Thumbprint Cookies (page 65). My Best Crescent Cookies (page 66) are enriched with brown rice flour that gives them unexpected tenderness and crunchiness. Italian Sweet Almond Amaretti Cookies (page 62) are so fragrant with a sweet almondy aroma; they are made with a handful of ingredients and are also oil free. I need to mention two favorites here for all the chocoholics: Wanna Be Brownie Cookies (page 50) and Chocolate Almond Butter Cookies (page 54). You will not be able to stop munching on these after taking the first chocolaty, melt-in-your-mouth bite.

WANNA BE BROWNIE COOKIES

YIELD: 16 COOKIES

These cookies are all about the good stuff. They are so soft, fudgy, rich and chocolaty that they will delight everyone. They are also easy to make and bake in no time. Enjoy them while they're warm and the chocolate is soft and melted for a true brownie experience. But be warned—these are quite addictive.

⅓ cup (80 ml) oat milk, room temperature

⅔ cup (90 g) coconut sugar

1 tbsp (15 g) golden flax seeds

3 tbsp (45 ml) water

½ cup (62 g) spelt flour (see Notes)

½ cup (70 g) brown rice flour

1 tsp baking powder

½ tsp vanilla powder or 1 tsp vanilla extract

2 pinches of salt

½ cup (50 g) unsweetened cocoa powder

¼ cup (50 g) almonds, finely ground (see Notes)

⅓ cup (80 ml) melted extra virgin coconut oil

⅓ cup (65 g) vegan chocolate chips or chopped vegan dark chocolate, divided

Preheat the oven to 355°F (180°C) on fan-assisted mode if possible, or conventional-baking mode if you don't have a fan-assisted oven.

In a large bowl, mix the milk with the sugar and stir until the sugar is dissolved. Grind the golden flax seeds in a coffee grinder or a small food processor until you achieve a fine meal; place the meal in a small bowl and mix it with the water until it starts to gel and resemble a beaten egg. Set it aside.

Sift the flours with the baking powder, vanilla, salt and cocoa powder into a large bowl. Add the ground almonds and combine. Mix, using a whisk, until all the ingredients are distributed evenly. Add the melted coconut oil to the milk-sugar mixture and whisk in the flax egg; add the wet ingredients to the dry ingredients. Gently fold the ingredients together. When you have a fairly homogenous dough, fold in two-thirds of the chocolate chips or chopped chocolate. Wrap the dough and place it in the refrigerator for 30 minutes to chill.

Line a large baking sheet with parchment paper. When the dough is chilled, use a small ice cream scoop to measure and place scoops of the dough on the sheet, leaving enough space in between the cookies, about 1½ inches (4 cm), so they can expand. Press them lightly to flatten, and decorate the top of each cookie with two to three pieces of chocolate.

Bake the cookies for 10 minutes on fan-assisted mode or 12 to 13 minutes on conventional-baking mode. When the time has elapsed, test the cookies by carefully sliding them around using the end of a spoon. If they're holding together, they're done. They will firm up as they cool down. Transfer the baking sheet onto a cooling rack and allow the cookies to cool for about 10 minutes. Then remove the cookies from the baking sheet and move them onto the cooling rack to allow them to cool down completely.

Once completely cooled, store the cookies in an airtight container at room temperature for up to 10 days.

NOTES: You can substitute brown rice flour for more spelt flour, if desired.

You can also use a heaping ⅓ cup (40 g) of almond meal instead of grinding your own almonds.

ALMOND COCONUT PALEO COOKIES

GLUTEN FREE; GRAIN FREE | YIELD: 14–16 COOKIES

These dense, coconutty cookies are a delicious grain-free dessert that are also a great grab-and-go treat or a quick snack. They are wonderfully chewy with a nice coconut and almond aroma in combination with intense dark chocolate chips, which makes them a delicious dessert. They're a protein-rich nutritional snack to have whenever you need a nourishing bite or a quick energy kick.

¼ cup (60 ml) oat milk, room temperature

1 tsp lemon juice

1½ cups (160 g) almond meal

½ cup (50 g) coconut flour

½ tsp baking soda

½ tsp baking powder

¼ tsp Himalayan salt

½ tsp vanilla powder or 1 tsp vanilla extract

½ cup (65 g) coconut sugar

2 tbsp (30 ml) agave or maple syrup

½ cup (120 ml) melted extra virgin coconut oil

⅓ cup (65 g) vegan dark chocolate chips, divided

Preheat the oven to 350°F (175°C).

Mix the milk with the lemon juice and set it aside to sour for 10 to 15 minutes.

To make the dough, in a large mixing bowl, sift the almond meal and coconut flour with the baking soda, baking powder, salt, vanilla and sugar. In a separate bowl, mix the agave syrup and oil. Add the wet ingredients to the dry ingredients and mix gently with a silicone spatula or a large wooden spoon. Gradually add the milk-lemon mixture and keep folding until you get a thick dough. Mix in the chocolate chips, reserving some for decorating the cookies. Refrigerate the dough for 15 minutes.

Line a large baking sheet with parchment paper. Using an ice cream scoop or a tablespoon, measure out the dough, shape it into discs and place them on the baking sheet, leaving some space in between to allow them to expand a bit.

Decorate them with more chocolate chips and bake on the middle rack for 8 minutes on conventional-baking mode, then switch to fan-assisted mode and bake another 6 to 7 minutes. Keep a close eye on them and check them after 5 to 6 minutes, since they can overbake easily.

They are done when nicely browned, still very soft but firm enough to move. They will firm up further as they cool down. Remove the cookies from the oven, and place the baking sheet on a cooling rack to cool for 10 to 15 minutes. Then gently transfer the cookies onto the cooling rack to cool down completely. You can have them freshly baked, but they will also keep nicely for a few days.

Store them in a sealed container for up to 10 days at room temperature or refrigerated. At room temperature the cookies will be super soft, while chilled cookies will be firmer and chewier.

CHOCOLATE ALMOND BUTTER COOKIES

GLUTEN FREE; GRAIN FREE | YIELD: 12 LARGE COOKIES

Melt in your mouth, super rich and chocolaty, these amazing cookies are little bites of paradise.
Super easy and quick to make, they are also gluten and grain free and protein rich, but they are so indulgent
that you'd never believe there was anything healthy and nutritious in them.

2 tbsp (30 g) golden flax seeds
6 tbsp (90 ml) water
1 cup (250 g) almond butter
⅓ cup (45 g) coconut sugar
¼ tsp salt
1 tsp vanilla extract
1 tbsp (15 ml) maple syrup
3 tbsp (30 g) unsweetened cocoa powder
½ tsp baking soda
⅓ cup (65 g) chocolate chunks, divided

Preheat the oven to 350°F (175°C). Line a large baking sheet with parchment paper. To make the flax eggs, grind the flaxseeds in a coffee grinder or a small food processor. Transfer the flax meal into a small bowl, add the water and mix until it starts to gel. Leave it aside to thicken.

In a large bowl, whisk the almond butter with the sugar, salt, vanilla and syrup until combined. Mix in the flax eggs. Sift the cocoa powder and baking soda into the bowl and fold with a silicone spatula until combined. Then add the chocolate chunks, reserving some for decorating the cookies. Refrigerate the dough for 15 minutes.

After the dough has chilled, use an ice cream scoop to measure the dough, shape it using your hands into discs, then place them onto the lined baking sheet, leaving 2 inches (5 cm) between cookies to allow them to expand. Decorate the cookies with more chocolate chunks.

Bake the cookies for 12 to 14 minutes, checking on them after 12 minutes have elapsed. If they can be moved and keep their shape, they are done. The cookies will still be very soft, but will firm up as they cool.

Transfer the baking sheet onto a cooling rack. After 10 minutes, carefully move the cookies from the baking sheet to the rack to cool for another 10 minutes. I love eating them freshly baked, even still warm, as they will be super soft and moist and those melted chocolate chunks are just delicious!

Store them in an airtight container, refrigerated, for up to 1 week.

FLOURLESS CHICKPEA ALMOND BUTTER COOKIES

GLUTEN FREE; GRAIN FREE | YIELD: 16 COOKIES

These delicious little treats are grain free and gluten free and rich in plant protein and fiber,
all because of the chickpeas and almonds. They're also super easy to make, and you can start
munching on them as soon as they're baked.

1⅓ cups (230 g) cooked or canned chickpeas

¼ cup (60 ml) maple syrup

½ cup (125 g) almond butter (see Note)

⅓ tsp salt

½ tsp baking powder

½ tsp vanilla powder or 1 tsp vanilla extract

⅓ cup (65 g) chopped vegan dark chocolate or vegan chocolate chips, divided

Preheat the oven to 340°F (170°C). Line a large baking sheet with parchment paper.

Rinse and drain the chickpeas well. If you prefer, remove the skins completely to make them easier to digest. Simply squeeze each chickpea gently and the skin will slide off.

Place all the ingredients except the chocolate chips in a food processor and blend until smooth. Using a silicone spatula, fold in the chocolate chips, reserving about a third. Using an ice cream scoop or a tablespoon, scoop out the batter and place it on the parchment paper–lined baking sheet, leaving enough space in between for the cookies to expand, about 2 inches (5 cm). Top each cookie with a few pieces of the remaining chocolate.

Bake them for 10 minutes on conventional-baking mode and another 5 minutes on fan-assisted mode. If fan-assisted mode isn't available, bake the cookies for another 2 to 3 minutes on conventional-baking mode. Leave them to cool for 10 to 15 minutes to allow them to firm up before lifting them off the paper and transferring them onto a wire rack to cool down completely.

These cookies are best eaten freshly baked, but they can also be stored in an airtight container for up to 4 days at room temperature or 7 days refrigerated.

NOTE: Feel free to use any other nut or seed butter of choice, but note that the flavor will be slightly different.

SWEET POTATO CHOCOLATE CHIP COOKIES

GLUTEN FREE; NUT FREE | YIELD: 16-18 COOKIES

These cookies are deliciously chewy and soft. Although they are gluten free, they are super easy to make and won't be falling apart. I love using sweet potato in desserts because it is a great way to add substance and sweetness to treats, while also adding some great nutritional value, since they're a great source of fiber, vitamins, minerals and good carbohydrates.

2 cups (270 g) peeled and cubed raw sweet potato

1¼ cups (160 g) brown rice flour

¾ cup (100 g) buckwheat flour

1 tbsp (10 g) tapioca starch

½ tsp baking powder

½ tsp baking soda

½ tsp fine Himalayan salt

¼ tsp cinnamon

½ tsp vanilla powder or 1 tsp vanilla extract

½ cup (120 ml) melted extra virgin coconut oil

½ cup (100 g) xylitol (see Note)

¼ cup (60 ml) agave syrup

½ cup (90 g) vegan dark chocolate chips, divided

Steam the sweet potato for 15 minutes or until tender and leave it to cool down completely.

Preheat the oven to 350°F (175°C) on conventional-baking mode.

In a large mixing bowl, sift the flours with the tapioca starch, baking powder, baking soda, salt, cinnamon and vanilla powder.

In a food processor, blend the peeled cooled sweet potato with the oil, xylitol and syrup until smooth.

Fold the mixture into the dry ingredients using a silicone spatula or a large wooden spoon until well incorporated. Next, fold in the chocolate chips, reserving ⅛ cup (23 g) for decorating the cookies. Refrigerate the cookie dough for 15 minutes.

Line a large baking sheet with parchment paper. Using a small ice cream scoop, scoop out the dough on the baking sheet, leaving some space in between; these cookies will not expand much. Gently press on each cookie to slightly flatten and decorate with the reserved chocolate chips.

Bake the cookies for 15 minutes on the middle rack until the edges of the cookies are nicely browned and they are firm enough to move. Remove them from the oven and place the baking sheet on a cooling rack to cool for about 10 minutes. Then gently transfer the cookies onto the cooling rack to cool down completely.

Store them in a sealed container at room temperature for up to 4 days or in the refrigerator for up to 10 days.

NOTE: You can substitute xylitol with the same amount of coconut sugar.

BLACK BEAN CHOCOLATE COOKIES

YIELD: 16 COOKIES

These chocolate cookies are such a great nutritious snack while also being a delicious dessert at the same time. They are soft and dense and almost creamy with a rich chocolate flavor that will satisfy even the pickiest of chocolate lovers. These delicious little bites are a nutritious bomb with a considerable amount of healthy plant protein, fats and fiber. For sweeter cookies, use ⅓ cup (80 ml) maple syrup; use ¼ cup (60 ml) if you prefer them less sweet.

---

1 cup (180 g) canned black beans (see Notes)

1 tbsp (15 g) flax seeds

3 tbsp (45 ml) water

3 tbsp (45 g) white spelt flour (see Notes)

1 tsp baking powder

Pinch of salt

4 tbsp (40 g) unsweetened cocoa powder

Pinch of cinnamon

½ tsp vanilla powder

⅓ cup (45 g) roasted hazelnuts (see Notes)

⅓ cup (50 g) cashews (see Notes)

3 tbsp (45 ml) melted extra virgin coconut oil

¼ to ⅓ cup (60 to 80 ml) maple syrup

1 tsp lemon juice

⅓ cup (65 g) chopped vegan chocolate or vegan chocolate chips

Preheat your oven to 350°F (175°C).

Wash the beans thoroughly and leave them to drain. When they're thoroughly drained, pat them dry to remove any bean flavor.

To make the flax egg, grind the flax seeds using a coffee bean grinder or a small food processor, mix them with the water in a small bowl and leave aside to thicken.

Sift the spelt flour, baking powder, salt, cocoa, cinnamon and vanilla into a large mixing bowl.

Finely grind the hazelnuts and cashews. Add them to the dry ingredients and mix to combine.

Place the drained beans in a food processor and add the oil, maple syrup and lemon juice. Blend until smooth.

Add the flax egg, bean mixture and chopped chocolate or chocolate chips into the dry ingredients. Mix gently until you get an even sticky dough. Using an ice cream scoop, scoop the batter onto a parchment paper–lined baking sheet. You can flatten them a bit or bake them as they are.

Bake the cookies for 15 minutes. After the time has elapsed, check if they're firm enough to move. If not, bake for another 2 to 3 minutes.

Leave them to cool for 15 to 20 minutes on the baking sheet, and transfer to the cooling rack to cool down completely. They are best enjoyed freshly baked, still warm.

Keep them in an airtight container in the refrigerator up to 1 week.

NOTES: Feel free to substitute the cashews and hazelnuts with almonds or any nut of choice.

For a gluten-free version, substitute spelt flour with buckwheat or brown rice flour.

I used black beans in this recipe, but you can also use brown or butter beans.

SWEET ALMOND AMARETTI COOKIES

GLUTEN FREE | YIELD: 16–18 COOKIES

These little cookies remind me so much of my childhood. My grandmother used to have store-bought amaretti cookies in the cupboard, and I loved sneaking into it and munching on them unseen. Whenever I taste that sweet almond flavor, I instantly feel like that little girl hiding behind the cupboard door again. This is my version, which is gluten free and oil free. I love the chewy texture and beautiful, powerful aroma of lemon zest and almond extract.

½ cup (85 g) almonds
½ cup (70 g) cashews
½ tsp lemon zest
1 tbsp (10 g) coconut sugar
2 tbsp (25 g) brown rice flour
1 tbsp (10 g) tapioca starch
Pinch of fine sea salt
½ tsp baking powder
2½ tbsp (38 ml) agave or maple syrup, divided
1 tbsp (15 ml) almond extract
½ to 1 tbsp (8 to 15 ml) water
3 tbsp (30 g) slivered/flaked almonds
½ tbsp (8 ml) almond milk

Preheat the oven to 300°F (150°C). Place the nuts in a baking dish and toast them for about 15 minutes or until slightly browned and fragrant.

Set them aside to cool. Increase the oven temperature to 355°F (180°C). Line a baking sheet with parchment paper.

Finely grind the cooled nuts and place them into a medium-sized bowl. Add the lemon zest, sugar, flour, tapioca starch, salt and baking powder. Mix using a silicone spatula.

In a small bowl, mix 2 tablespoons (30 ml) of syrup and almond extract with ½ tablespoon (8 ml) of water. Add to the dry ingredients, folding with a spatula to incorporate the ingredients until you get a dough consistency. If the dough feels too dry, add another ½ tablespoon (8 ml) of water.

Place the slivered almonds into a small bowl. Using your fingers, shape walnut-sized pieces of dough into balls, and flatten them gently to get a disc shape. In a small cup, whisk together the milk and remaining ½ tablespoon (8 ml) of syrup and brush the discs, pop them into a bowl with the almonds and press gently to get the almond flakes to stick.

Place the cookies on the baking sheet, about 1 inch (2.5 cm) apart. Place the baking sheet in the oven and bake for 10 to 12 minutes. They are done when they are slightly browned and hold their shape when gently moved.

Transfer the baking sheet to the cooling rack, and as soon as the cookies are cooled enough, move and transfer them onto the wire rack to cool down completely.

Store them in the sealed container at room temperature for up to 2 weeks.

BUTTERY ALMOND THUMBPRINT COOKIES

GLUTEN FREE | YIELD: 24 COOKIES

Thumbprint cookies have always been my little family's Christmas classic, partly because there isn't any dough kneading, rolling or cutting pastry involved. And partly because I just love buttery vanilla cookie and jam flavors together. My thumbprint cookie recipes have changed over time. I started by using a conventional recipe I learned from my mother that calls for refined ingredients like bleached wheat flour, sugar and butter. Then I subbed the white sugar with brown sugar and progressed to using even more wholesome sweeteners and all-vegan ingredients. I replaced the bleached wheat flour first with unbleached, then finally swapped it to more nutritious grain flours and nuts. This is my latest incredibly buttery and delicious version, which also happens to be gluten free.

½ cup plus 1 tbsp (135 g) chilled vegan butter

¼ cup (33 g) coconut sugar

2 tbsp (30 ml) agave or maple syrup

⅔ cup (78 g) almond flour

¼ tsp salt

1 tsp vanilla powder

3 tbsp (30 g) tapioca starch

1 cup (130 g) brown rice flour

4 tbsp (30 g) flaked almonds

4 tbsp (100 g) smooth raspberry jam

Preheat the oven to 355°F (180°C) and line a baking sheet with parchment paper.

In a large bowl, beat the butter, sugar and syrup. Sift in the almond flour, salt, vanilla, tapioca starch and rice flour. Mix well until the mixture forms a soft, doughy consistency.

Place the flaked almonds in a small bowl and set aside.

To shape the cookies, measure the dough with a tablespoon-sized (15-g) measuring scoop, and roll it into balls. Roll them in the flaked almonds, and place them on a baking sheet about 2 inches (5 cm) apart. Using your thumb or the back of ½-teaspoon measuring spoon, gently press the top of each ball to make an indentation in the center of each cookie. If you want, pinch together large cracks around the sides of each to get neater cookies. Fill each indentation with ½ teaspoon of raspberry jam.

Bake the cookies for 10 to 12 minutes. When done, the cookies will brown slightly on the bottom and will still hold their shape when moved. They will harden as they cool down, so be careful not to overbake them.

Transfer the baking sheet onto a cooling rack. As soon as the cookies are cool enough, move them to the rack to cool completely.

Store them in a sealed container on the countertop for up to 3 to 4 days or in the refrigerator for up to 1 week.

THE BEST CRESCENT COOKIES

YIELD: 26 COOKIES

So light and crunchy, these are my family's absolute favorite Christmas cookie. These have been made so many times in my workshops and by my friends; they have always been met with rave reviews as "the best crescent cookie recipe" out there, and I agree! What makes them special and incredibly crunchy is the addition of brown rice flour. They can keep pretty long and can be made up to two weeks in advance, so there's that too.

¼ cup (40 g) brown rice flour

½ cup (65 g) white spelt flour

2 tbsp (20 g) tapioca starch

Pinch of fine Himalayan salt

¼ tsp vanilla powder or ½ tsp vanilla extract

1 cup (110 g) almond meal

3 tbsp (60 g) vegan butter

3 tbsp (45 ml) agave syrup

2 tbsp (20 g) powdered xylitol, for sifting (see Note)

Preheat the oven to 325°F (160°C) and line two large baking sheets with parchment paper.

Sift the flours, tapioca starch, salt and vanilla into a large bowl. Add the almond meal and whisk to combine. In a separate bowl, whisk together the butter and syrup until nice and fluffy. Add these to the dry ingredients and fold gently using a silicone spatula or a large wooden spoon until a dough is formed. If needed, use your hands to knead lightly and briefly to shape a dough. Wrap the dough in plastic wrap and refrigerate for at least 30 minutes.

To shape the cookies, take small bits of dough, roll them into 1-inch (2.5-cm) balls and then shape the balls into 2½-inch (6-cm)-long logs. Pinch the ends of the logs to taper them and turn the ends in slightly, forming crescents. The sizes are approximate; the cookies can be slightly bigger or smaller. Place the cookies on the baking sheets, spacing them 1 inch (2.5 cm) apart.

Bake each sheet separately; bake them until the cookies are light brown around the edges and firm to the touch, about 15 minutes. Cool the cookies for about 10 minutes on the baking sheets.

Sprinkle the xylitol on top of the crescents, transfer and cool them completely on cooling racks. Cookies can be prepared up to 2 weeks ahead and stored at room temperature in an airtight container. They will last for up to 1 month.

NOTE: You can substitute the xylitol with tapioca starch mixed with a pinch of vanilla powder.

CHOCOLATE BLISS

Chocolate is a sweet (and sometimes guilt-inducing) addiction for many of us. Luckily, when it comes in the form of wholesome, plant-based desserts like the ones featured in this chapter, satisfying your chocolate cravings can be blissful and guilt free!

Chocolate goes beautifully with wholesome ingredients like coconut oil, maple syrup and rice and spelt flours. It also magically masks the taste of legumes like beans and chickpeas or veggies like sweet potato and zucchini that are a healthy, vegan way to get the creamy, fudgy, moist texture that we all want in our desserts. It is quite incredible how beans make beautifully creamy parfaits and fluffy brownies, or how grated zucchini or apple adds moisture to baked spongy cakes without influencing the mouthwatering chocolate flavor.

This "Chocolate Bliss" chapter will help you make decadent, rich chocolate desserts that will blow your mind with deep chocolate flavor, but that could be considered a wholesome meal or snack at the same time. Recipes like the Fudgiest Bakery-Style Brownies (page 70), Amazing Sweet Potato Brownies (page 77) or Luscious Triple Chocolate Tart (page 73) will become some of your favorites.

Just a word of warning—they are quite addictive. All these desserts are easy to make, both in terms of the number of ingredients used and simplicity of the methods. They will require less than 30 minutes of your time and just one or two bowls to prepare.

If you're in a search of an impressive, more complicated chocolate dessert, take a look in the "Decadent Cakes" chapter (page 13) for more inspiration. I'm quite confident that some of the recipes featured in it—including The Chocolate Cake (page 14) or Sacher Torte (page 20)—could satisfy even the pickiest chocolate lovers out there.

FUDGIEST BAKERY–STYLE BROWNIES

GLUTEN FREE; NUT FREE | YIELD: 9 BROWNIES

This must be one of my absolute favorite chocolate desserts of all time. These brownies are so incredibly fudgy. They literally melt in your mouth, and they taste like they're loaded with eggs, butter and sugar, even though they're made with healthier vegan ingredients. They're ultra-indulgent and almost too good to be true, but the recipe is super quick and easy. I am quite sure that you'll be amazed by the result you'll achieve with these simple wholesome ingredients.

1 leveled cup (130 g) brown rice flour

⅔ cup (65 g) unsweetened cocoa powder

1 tbsp (10 g) tapioca starch

⅓ tsp Himalayan salt

½ tsp baking powder

½ cup (65 g) coconut sugar

1 cup (240 ml) hot water

½ cup (120 ml) melted extra virgin coconut oil

1½ tsp (8 ml) lemon juice

¼ to ⅓ cup (50 to 65 g) vegan dark chocolate chips or chopped vegan chocolate, divided

Preheat the oven to 350°F (175°C) and prepare a 7-inch (18-cm) square ceramic baking dish. Grease the bottom and sides, and line it with parchment paper.

Sift the flour, cocoa powder, tapioca starch, salt and baking powder into a medium-sized mixing bowl and mix, using a whisk to evenly distribute the ingredients.

In a small bowl, whisk the sugar with the hot water to dissolve it and leave to cool. Once the sugar and water have cooled down to warm but not hot, make a well in the dry ingredients and add the sugar-water mixture, oil and lemon juice. Fold gently to combine, then whisk to get the batter smooth. Add the chocolate chips, reserving a few pieces to decorate the brownies.

Transfer the batter into the prepared baking dish, gently shake to level and smooth the top. Scatter the reserved chocolate on top and bake for 20 minutes. When the brownies are done, the center will still seem a little undone and wobbly, but it will set in the pan while it cools down.

Let the brownies cool down completely before slicing. Store the brownies in an airtight container and refrigerate for up to 10 days.

If you serve them directly from the refrigerator, they will be firm and resemble a chocolate bar; when served at room temperature, they will be incredibly fudgy and soft.

LUSCIOUS TRIPLE CHOCOLATE TART

GLUTEN FREE | YIELD: 1 (9-INCH [23-CM]) TART; 12 SLICES

Now that I said "triple chocolate," is there any need for further information about this delicious, chocolaty tart? Let me say it anyway: This tart features a crunchy baked almond and buckwheat crust topped with an intensely dark chocolate layer and a lusciously sweet, smooth and fluffy potato ganache filling. It is so rich and chocolaty. Simply divine!

CRUST

1 cup (100 g) old fashioned rolled oats (see Notes)

1 cup (135 g) almonds

½ cup (70 g) buckwheat flour

2 tbsp (20 g) unsweetened cocoa

¼ tsp fine Himalayan salt

¼ tsp vanilla powder or 1 tsp vanilla extract

¼ cup (60 ml) melted extra virgin coconut oil

3 tbsp (45 ml) maple syrup

1 tsp lemon juice

CHOCOLATE

3 tbsp (30 g) extra virgin coconut oil

3 tbsp (45 ml) maple syrup

5 tbsp (50 g) unsweetened cocoa powder

⅓ cup (80 ml) oat or almond milk, room temperature

CHOCOLATE SWEET POTATO GANACHE FILLING

2 tbsp (30 g) unrefined cocoa butter

1 cup (185 g) steamed sweet potato

½ cup (120 ml) almond or oat milk, room temperature

Pinch of Himalayan salt

½ tsp lemon juice

⅓ cup (30 g) unsweetened cocoa powder

1 tbsp (30 g) cashew butter

OPTIONAL TOPPING

Fresh berries

Preheat the oven to 350°F (175°C). Lightly grease a 9-inch (23-cm) tart pan with a removable bottom (see Notes).

To prepare the crust, place the oats in a food processor and grind them finely. Set them aside, add the almonds to the food processor and grind roughly. Don't grind them too finely, as we want some bite left to them. Return the ground oats to the food processor with the almonds, and add the rest of the crust ingredients. Process and pulse until you get a wet dough that sticks when pressed between your fingers. Transfer it into the prepared pan and form the crust by pressing it into the bottom and onto the sides. Bake the crust for about 12 minutes, or until the crust is fragrant, firm to the touch and lightly browned around the edges (see Notes). Leave it to cool on the cooling rack.

To make the chocolate, place the oil and syrup in a double boiler. Melt and add the cocoa powder. Using a whisk, stir until smooth. Add the milk gradually, continuously whisking until you achieve a smooth consistency again. Pour the chocolate over the cooled crust and shake the pan to smooth and level the chocolate. Place it into the refrigerator to set.

To make the sweet potato filling, melt the cocoa butter in a double boiler and set it aside to cool. Add the sweet potato, milk, salt, lemon juice and melted cocoa butter to a high-speed blender and blend until smooth. Next, add the cocoa powder and cashew butter and keep blending until smooth and creamy.

Pour the sweet potato ganache over the cooled chocolate layer. Gently shake the pan to level the filling. Use a silicone spatula to smooth it or make a swirl.

Chill the tart in the refrigerator for at least 2 hours before serving. Serve it straight out of the refrigerator, or decorate it with some fresh berries, if using.

NOTES: This tart crust doesn't have to be baked. It is up to you. Bake it for a crunchier result or leave it raw.

To ensure these are gluten free, be sure to use certified gluten-free oats in the recipe.

If you don't have a tart pan with a removable bottom, you can also use a regular pan, but it will be slightly harder to take it out.

SWEET POTATO BOUNTY TRUFFLES

GRAIN FREE; GLUTEN FREE | YIELD: 35–40 TRUFFLES

These delicious little treats are pure bliss. I consider them a more wholesome and nutritious version of the Bounty Bars that I adored as a kid. I promise they won't disappoint you, even if you were as big a fan as I was. The coconut center is beautifully creamy and the dark chocolate coating surrounds it with an intense chocolate flavor. Feel free to substitute almonds with other nuts at your disposal. If you don't feel like making the chocolate yourself, you can use store-bought vegan dark chocolate. Simply melt it in a double boiler with 1 to 2 tablespoons (15 to 30 ml) of plant milk and coat the truffles as instructed.

TRUFFLES

1 large sweet potato

1 cup (150 g) almonds

1 cup (75 g) shredded coconut

3 tbsp (45 ml) melted extra virgin coconut oil

2 tbsp (30 ml) lemon juice

2 to 3 tbsp (30 to 45 ml) maple or agave syrup

HOMEMADE DARK CHOCOLATE COATING

3 tbsp (30 g) extra virgin coconut oil

3 tbsp (45 ml) maple or agave syrup

5 tbsp (50 g) unsweetened cocoa powder

⅓ cup (80 ml) oat or almond milk, room temperature

NOTE: You can make a double-chocolate version of these truffles by simply adding 4 tablespoons (40 g) of unsweetened cocoa to the dough before chilling it. You will get intensely chocolate truffles with a creamy chocolate center and dark chocolate coating to satisfy even the biggest of chocolate addicts. I myself love both versions equally and usually divide the dough into two parts and make both versions simultaneously.

Preheat the oven to 350°F (175°C). Wash the sweet potato, pat it dry and, using a fork, pierce the skin all around. Place it on a baking sheet lined with parchment paper and bake for 45 to 50 minutes. When done, it should be very soft to the touch and be easily pierced with a fork. Leave it to cool down enough to peel off the skin. Place it in a bowl and mash it with a fork until smooth. Measure out 1½ cups (360 g).

Finely grind the almonds and add them to the mashed sweet potato. Add the coconut, oil, lemon juice and syrup. Using a spatula, mix the ingredients until combined and a dough has formed. Store in the refrigerator for at least 1 hour to firm up.

Once chilled, use your hands to make walnut-sized pieces of dough and shape them into balls. Place them in a closed container, or cover on a plate and leave them in the refrigerator overnight to cool. If you're in a time crunch, you can chill them in the freezer for 1 hour instead.

To prepare the chocolate coating, add the oil and syrup to a small bowl placed over a pot of boiling water (the double boiler method). When the oil is completely melted, add the cocoa powder and keep mixing for about 30 seconds, until you get a smooth liquid consistency. Gradually add the milk, continuously mixing for another 30 seconds. The chocolate will first thicken, but then it will smooth down again as you keep mixing it. In the end, you should get a nice, smooth and shiny chocolate sauce.

Dip each truffle into the liquid chocolate using two forks. When they're evenly coated, take them out and place them on parchment paper, making sure to keep them apart so they don't stick together. When done, return them to the refrigerator for another 30 minutes for the chocolate coating to firm up completely. If you would like to make these truffles even prettier, after the chocolate coating has firmed up, you can drizzle them with more chocolate and place them back into the refrigerator to cool again.

Keep the truffles in a closed container in the refrigerator for up to 10 days or for up to 2 months in the freezer.

AMAZING SWEET POTATO BROWNIES

GLUTEN FREE | YIELD: 12 BROWNIES

Rich, intensely chocolaty and indulgent, with a rich and creamy sweet potato frosting, these brownies are a chocolate bomb that will impress anyone. I recommend making them at least a day in advance, as they get better in the following days.

BROWNIES

1 tbsp (15 g) golden flax seeds

3 tbsp (45 ml) water

1 cup (240 ml) almond milk, room temperature

2 tsp (10 ml) apple cider vinegar

⅔ cup (100 g) buckwheat flour (see Note)

1 tbsp (10 g) tapioca starch

½ tsp baking soda

½ tsp baking powder

¼ tsp fine Himalayan salt

1 tsp vanilla powder or 2 tsp (10 ml) vanilla extract

7 tbsp (70 g) unsweetened cocoa powder

⅓ cup (35 g) almond meal

½ tbsp (7 g) chia seeds

½ cup (125 g) sweet potato puree

⅓ cup plus 1 tbsp (95 ml) maple syrup

¼ cup (60 ml) melted extra virgin coconut oil

2 tsp (10 ml) lemon juice

CHOCOLATE SWEET POTATO FROSTING

2 tbsp (18 g) unrefined cocoa butter

1 cup (185 g) steamed sweet potato

½ cup (120 ml) almond or oat milk, room temperature

Pinch of Himalayan salt

½ tsp lemon juice

⅓ cup (35 g) unsweetened cocoa powder

1 tbsp (30 g) cashew butter

Preheat the oven to 350°F (175°C) and prepare an 8-inch (20-cm) square pan by greasing it and lining the bottom with parchment paper, leaving the sides to overlap to easily remove the brownies. Grind the flax seeds using a coffee bean grinder or a small food processor to make the flax egg. Mix with the water in a small bowl and leave it aside to thicken. Mix the milk with the apple cider vinegar and set it aside to sour for 10 to 15 minutes.

Sift the flour with the tapioca starch, baking soda, baking powder, salt, vanilla and cocoa powder into a large mixing bowl. Add the almond meal and chia seeds and mix. In a separate bowl, whisk together the sweet potato puree, syrup, oil and lemon juice.

Make a well in the dry ingredients and add the sweet potato mixture and flax egg. Fold it gently with a silicone spatula or a large wooden spoon. Pour in the soured milk and keep folding gently until just combined. Do not overmix. Transfer the batter into the prepared baking pan, and shake it gently to level and smooth the surface with a spatula if needed.

Bake the brownies for 20 to 24 minutes. At the 20-minute mark, check if the brownies are done by piercing the center all the way through with a toothpick. If it comes out almost clean, with just a trace of chocolate on it, they're done. If it's covered in wet batter, keep baking for another 4 minutes and check again.

When done, the center can still look slightly undercooked, but it will set while cooling in the pan. Take the brownies out of the oven and place the pan on a cooling rack. Leave it to cool down completely before frosting.

To make the sweet potato frosting, melt the cocoa butter in a double boiler. Leave it to cool and then add it to a high-speed blender with the sweet potato, milk, salt and lemon juice. Blend until smooth. Add the cocoa powder and cashew butter. Keep blending until smooth and creamy. Transfer the frosting into a container and refrigerate for at least 30 minutes to set. Use it to frost the brownies before cutting them into squares and serving.

You can store them in a sealed container or wrapped tightly in the refrigerator for up to 1 week. I recommend taking them out of the refrigerator 15 to 20 minutes before serving to soften.

NOTE: If you can't find buckwheat flour, you can use white whole wheat, white spelt, brown rice or all-purpose unbleached flour. Follow the amounts in cups, as they all weigh differently in grams.

BLACK BEAN CHOCOLATE MOUSSE

GLUTEN FREE; GRAIN FREE | YIELD: 4 SMALL (4-OZ [120-ML]) JARS

Super decadent and so chocolaty you wouldn't believe it was also healthy and wholesome, this dessert is also protein rich, gluten free, refined sugar free and vegan. You will not taste the beans because they are perfectly masked in roasted hazelnut and chocolate flavors, but they give an amazing creamy texture to this dessert and so much nutritious goodness.

1⅓ cups (240 g) cooked black beans

½ cup (120 ml) plus 1 tbsp (15 ml) oat or almond milk, at room temperature, divided

½ cup (65 g) roasted hazelnuts

2 tbsp (30 ml) melted extra virgin coconut oil

3 to 4 tbsp (45 to 60 ml) maple or agave syrup

Pinch of salt

1 tsp lemon juice

½ tsp vanilla powder or 1 tsp vanilla extract

3 to 4 tbsp (30 to 40 g) unsweetened cocoa powder

OPTIONAL TOPPING
Coconut Whipped Cream (page 25)

Drain and rinse the beans and pat them dry to get rid of any beany flavor. Place them in a blender with ½ cup (120 ml) of the milk, hazelnuts, oil, syrup, salt, lemon juice and vanilla. Blend until very smooth and creamy. Add the cocoa powder and continue blending. If the mixture is too thick for your blender, add a tablespoon (15 ml) of milk or use a spatula to mix in the cocoa.

Divide the mousse between the jars and store in the refrigerator to chill well before serving. You can top them with Coconut Whipped Cream, if using, for an even more luscious dessert.

CHOCOLATE PROTEIN BANANA BREAD

YIELD: 1 (9 X 5-INCH [23 X 13-CM]) LOAF

Intensely rich, chocolaty and moist, this banana bread is not only nutritious and protein rich, thanks to added vegan protein, but also a delicious treat that will satisfy all the chocolate lovers out there. Serve it with a drizzle of peanut butter for even more protein intake and even more delicious richness.

1 tbsp (15 g) golden flax seeds

3 tbsp (45 ml) water

½ cup (70 g) brown rice flour

½ cup (62 g) white spelt flour

1 tsp baking powder

½ tsp baking soda

⅓ tsp Himalayan salt

5 tbsp (50 g) unsweetened cocoa powder

2 tbsp (30 g) chocolate or vanilla flavored vegan protein powder

1 tsp vanilla extract or ½ tsp vanilla powder

3 very ripe bananas, peeled

⅓ cup (80 ml) melted extra virgin coconut oil

⅓ cup (80 ml) agave or maple syrup

1 tsp lemon juice

1 tsp apple cider vinegar

½ cup (55 g) walnuts

⅓ cup (65 g) vegan chocolate chips or chopped vegan dark chocolate, divided

1 banana

½ tsp coconut sugar, for decoration

OPTIONAL TOPPINGS

Peanut butter

Fresh berries

Preheat the oven to 350°F (175°C) on fan-assisted mode. Arrange a rack in the bottom third of the oven and line a 9 x 5-inch (23 x 13–cm) loaf pan with parchment paper, letting the excess hang over the long sides.

Grind the flax seeds and place them in a small bowl; add the water and mix to make the flax egg.

In a large mixing bowl, sift the flours with the baking powder, baking soda, salt, cocoa powder, protein powder and vanilla.

In a food processor, blend the ripe bananas with the oil, syrup, lemon juice and vinegar.

Add the banana mixture and flax egg to the dry ingredients. Using a silicone spatula or a large wooden spoon, gently stir until the ingredients are just barely combined. It's okay if you can see a few traces of flour. Chop the walnuts and chocolate and fold them into the batter, reserving a few pieces of chocolate for decoration.

Pour the batter into the prepared loaf pan and smooth out the top of the batter using a spatula or spoon. Slice the banana in half lengthwise and sprinkle a little coconut sugar on the cut sides of the banana. Gently arrange the banana slices on top of the batter, sugared side up and very gently press it into the batter. Add the reserved pieces of chocolate.

Bake in the preheated oven for 30 minutes on fan-assisted mode, or until a toothpick inserted into the center comes out mostly clean. If you bake it on conventional-baking mode, you will probably need to extend the cook time to 40 to 45 minutes. Once baked, transfer the pan to a wire rack and let it cool.

Serve it with a drizzle of peanut butter and berries, if using, for even more protein and deliciousness.

To store, place your banana bread in an airtight container or wrap it tightly in plastic wrap. Leave it on the countertop for up to 4 days or refrigerate for up to 1 week. You can also freeze it for up to 3 to 4 months. If you freeze the whole loaf, allow it to defrost on the countertop for 2 to 3 hours. If you freeze individual slices, defrost them on the countertop for 20 to 30 minutes.

DARK CHOCOLATE CHIA MUFFINS

YIELD: 12 MUFFINS

These muffins are so rich and super chocolaty that I just had to include them in this chapter. They taste amazing all by themselves, especially if you're a fan of intense dark chocolate flavor. But I have got to say, I love them with some nut butter and tangy fruit jam to give them an extra punch of deliciousness.

1 tbsp (15 g) golden flax seeds

3 tbsp (45 ml) water

½ cup (120 ml) almond milk, room temperature

1 tsp apple cider vinegar

½ cup (70 g) brown rice flour

½ cup (62 g) white spelt flour

1 tsp baking soda

¼ tsp salt

1 tsp vanilla powder or 2 tsp (10 ml) vanilla extract

4 tbsp (40 g) unsweetened cocoa powder

1 tbsp (12 g) chia seeds

⅓ cup (80 ml) maple or agave syrup (see Notes)

⅓ cup (80 ml) melted extra virgin coconut oil

⅓ cup (85 g) grated apple

OPTIONAL

⅓ cup (65 g) vegan dark chocolate chips

Peanut butter

Raspberry jam

Preheat the oven to 355°F (180°C). Line a 12-cup muffin pan with silicone or paper liners. If using paper liners, grease them with some melted coconut oil to prevent them from sticking.

Grind the flax seeds and mix them with the water in a small bowl. Set it aside to allow to thicken.

Mix the milk with the apple cider vinegar and leave it to sour for 10 to 15 minutes.

In a large bowl, sift the flours, baking soda, salt, vanilla and cocoa powder. Add the chia seeds and mix. In a smaller bowl, mix the syrup and oil, and add the mixture and the flax egg to the dry ingredients. Fold gently with a silicone spatula or a large wooden spoon. Pour in the soured milk and keep folding gently until just combined. Add the grated apple and fold in. The batter should be lumpy instead of smooth. Don't overmix. If using, fold in the chocolate chips.

Evenly divide the batter into the muffin cups, about 2 tablespoons (30 ml) for each muffin. The cups should be two-thirds full.

Bake in the oven for about 15 minutes, until the muffins have a nice dome and are slightly cracked on the top. Check if they're done by inserting a toothpick in the middle. It should come out almost clean, with just a few moist crumbs attached.

Remove the muffins from the oven and allow them to cool slightly in the pan for about 3 to 5 minutes, then transfer them onto a wire rack. This will prevent them from overcooking. Let them cool for about 20 minutes and enjoy them warm.

You can store the muffins in a closed container at room temperature for up to 3 days.

NOTES: I prefer baking the muffins and cupcakes in silicone liners or in a greased and floured muffin pan. You can use paper cups, but be sure to grease them to prevent sticking.

These muffins are not on the sweet side, but if you'd like them to be, increase the amount of syrup by 2 tablespoons (30 ml).

SUPER CHOCOLATY ZUCCHINI BREAD

YIELD: 1 (9 X 5-INCH [23 X 13-CM]) LOAF

Super chocolaty and moist, this zucchini bread is a delicious way to get more veggies into your diet, especially for your children's diets, since you won't taste the zucchini, just chocolate and almonds. Have it as a dessert or a snack, or even as a decadent but healthy breakfast. I recommend you try it with some nut butter and tangy fruits like berries to make it even more of a delicious and nutritious meal.

⅔ cup plus 2 tbsp (190 ml) oat milk, at room temperature

1 tsp apple cider vinegar

2 tbsp (30 g) golden flax seeds

6 tbsp (90 ml) water

1 cup (125 g) white spelt flour

½ tsp baking powder

½ tsp baking soda

⅓ tsp Himalayan salt

4 tbsp (40 g) unsweetened cocoa powder

½ tsp vanilla powder or 1 tsp vanilla extract

½ cup (55 g) ground almonds

½ cup (120 ml) melted extra virgin coconut oil

⅓ cup (80 ml) agave syrup

1 tsp lemon juice

⅔ cup (140 g) grated and squeezed zucchini, about 1 medium zucchini

⅓ cup (65 g) vegan chocolate chips or chopped vegan dark chocolate, divided

OPTIONAL TOPPINGS

Nut butter of choice

Fresh berries

Homemade Dark Chocolate Coating (page 74)

Preheat the oven to 350°F (175°C) on conventional-baking mode.

Arrange the rack in the bottom third of the oven. Grease and line a 9 x 5-inch (23 x 13-cm) loaf pan with parchment paper, letting the excess hang over the long sides to ease the removal of the bread once baked.

Mix the milk with the apple cider vinegar and set it aside to sour for 10 to 15 minutes. Grind the golden flax seeds in a coffee bean grinder or a small food processor, then place it in a small bowl and mix with the water for a flax egg. Set it aside to thicken.

In a large mixing bowl, sift the flour with baking powder, baking soda, salt, cocoa powder and vanilla. Add the almonds and whisk to evenly incorporate the dry ingredients and get rid of any lumps.

Mix the oil, syrup and lemon juice in a small bowl, add the flax egg and pour it into the dry ingredients. Fold gently. Add the soured milk, and using a silicone spatula or a large wooden spoon, gently fold until the ingredients are just barely combined. It's okay if you can see a few traces of flour. Do not overmix. Fold in the grated and squeezed zucchini and chocolate chips, reserving a small amount of chocolate for the top of the bread.

Pour the batter into the prepared loaf pan and smooth out the top of the batter using a spatula or a spoon. Arrange more chocolate on top and press it gently into the batter.

Bake the bread in the preheated oven for 40 minutes, or until a toothpick inserted into the center comes out mostly clean. When done, transfer the pan to a wire rack and cool for 10 to 15 minutes. Then remove the bread from the pan and leave it on the rack to cool down completely. To serve, slice the bread and top the slices with some of the suggested toppings, if using, for even more deliciousness.

Store the bread in an airtight container or wrap it tightly in plastic wrap and leave it on the countertop for up to 4 days. You can refrigerate it for up to 1 week. You can also freeze the bread for up to 3 months. If you freeze the whole loaf, allow it to defrost on the countertop for 2 to 3 hours before serving. If you freeze individual slices, defrost them on the countertop for 20 to 30 minutes before serving.

CHOCOLATE *and* HAZELNUT PARFAITS

GLUTEN FREE | YIELD: 3 CUPS (720 ML)

This vegan chocolate parfait is such a light dessert while also being a super chocolaty indulgence that will not only nourish your soul but also your body. I've served many of these delicious parfaits for dinner parties, and no one ever guessed that they were made with anything remotely healthy! Trust me, they are as decadent as the heavy cream-based desserts made with dairy, butter or eggs, with one huge distinction—these will leave you happy and light, as opposed to feeling sluggish and, in my case, nauseous. They're packed with super healthy ingredients like whole grain rice, chia seeds, coconut oil and cocoa while also being refined sugar free, gluten free and darn delicious. I should mention that these are super easy to make and will only take you ten minutes to make if you already have cooked rice on hand.

1¼ cups (225 g) cooked whole grain rice

1¼ to 1½ cups (300 to 360 ml) oat milk, at room temperature

3 tbsp (60 g) hazelnut butter

1 tbsp (12 g) chia seeds

1 tbsp (10 g) coconut sugar

2 tbsp (30 ml) agave syrup

1 tbsp (15 ml) melted extra virgin coconut oil

⅓ tsp vanilla powder or ½ tsp vanilla extract

Pinch of salt

½ tbsp (8 ml) lemon juice

4 tbsp (40 g) unsweetened cocoa powder

OPTIONAL TOPPINGS

Coconut Whipped Cream (page 25)

Extra unsweetened cocoa powder

Chopped vegan chocolate

Chopped roasted hazelnuts

Place the rice and milk in a blender, starting with 1¼ cups (300 ml) of milk, and blend until smooth. Add the hazelnut butter, chia seeds, sugar, syrup, oil, vanilla, salt and lemon juice, and continue blending. If it's too thick to blend, add more milk by the tablespoon (15 ml) until smooth. Add the cocoa powder and blend until the cream is very silky and smooth.

Pour it into the cups or jars of your choice and place them in the refrigerator for at least a few hours to set. You can serve them with some Coconut Whipped Cream, sifted with extra unsweetened cocoa powder or topped with some chopped chocolate and hazelnuts, if using.

You can store the parfaits in the closed jars for up to 4 days.

FRUITY GALETTES
AND CRUMBLES

This chapter is all about easy, fuss-free fruity goodness. These simple, stress-free recipes involve tender and juicy fruit fillings and either a crunchy buttery galette crust or crunchy crumble topping. These desserts are meant to be beautiful but a little messy and imperfect.

Galettes are my summer love. This rustic, pie-like summer dessert is a simple, delicious, crunchy pastry wrapped around fresh fruit. It's a lot like a fruit pie, but with a lot less effort. Seriously, turning summer fruit into a galette will make you feel like a kitchen pro. I don't even bother making regular pies anymore, because galettes are easier to make and don't even need a baking pan to create an amazing result. Also, I'm a little too lazy to make conventional pies in a pie dish and everything.

Crumbles are ridiculously simple to make and are as wholesome a dessert as you can get. They are basically seasoned fruits topped with oats and baked, creating delicious flavors of bursting, soft, fruity bases and crunchy baked streusel toppings.

All the galette and crumble recipes are flexible in terms of filling and crust/crumble topping. Feel free to use any combination, either because you prefer some or because you have all the ingredients on hand.

BEFORE YOU GET STARTED

Rules for making the most gorgeous galettes:

- Everything used to make a crust pastry has to be chilled; this includes your utensils, bowls and even your hands.

- The coconut oil, vegan butter and water also have to be very cold. The pastry dough does not have to be kneaded. Work with it very briefly just to get the ingredients to stick together in a dough.

- All the galette recipes are flexible in terms of using coconut oil or vegan butter; you can use either. Coconut oil is slightly more difficult to work with, but I love the result so much more! The crust will be flakier and crunchier. Coconut oil is a natural, wholesome ingredient, while vegan butter can be a highly processed one. As I mentioned, vegan butter is the only arguably "unhealthy" ingredient I use in this book. Be sure to use the one without trans-fats or any other highly processed ingredients. Always check the labels, and if possible go for the organic products.

- I added tapioca starch to all the galette fillings, because it will absorb the juices flowing out of fruits while baking and makes the fillings thick instead of making the crusts soggy. For the same reason, please do not include any of the juice released by the fruits before baking. Tapioca can be replaced by corn or arrowroot starch if you have those on hand instead.

Rules for making the most scrumptious crumbles:

- I prefer using old-fashioned rolled oats, not quick oats, as I don't like the topping mushy or soft, which can happen with quick oats because they absorb much more liquid.

- Sweeten the fruits to your liking. We're all different in that way.

- You can use almost any fruits of your liking, but be sure to cut them into small or thin enough pieces. Firmer fruits like apple and pear will cook too long if they're left in too big of pieces.

PEACH *and* BLACKBERRY GALETTE

NUT FREE | YIELD: 6-8 SLICES

This galette spells summer. I always go a bit crazy when blackberries and peaches are in season, and this delicious treat is one of my favorites to make. It's easy, it's quick and it's so tasty with its rich fruity center and a delicious spelt flour and coconut oil crust. For even more deliciousness, add a scoop of vegan vanilla ice cream on top and let it melt slightly for the ultimate sweet indulgence.

CRUST

½ cup (100 g) vegan butter or ½ cup (120 ml) melted extra virgin coconut oil

1 cup plus 1 tbsp (140 g) white spelt flour

½ tsp cinnamon

⅓ tsp salt

1½ tbsp (15 g) coconut sugar

4 to 5 tbsp (60 to 75 ml) ice water

1 tbsp (10 g) tapioca starch

FILLING

1½ cups (180 g) blackberries

1 tbsp (10 g) tapioca starch

1 tsp cinnamon, divided

2 tbsp (30 ml) agave syrup

2 cups (250 g) thinly sliced peach

3 tbsp (30 g) coconut sugar, divided (see Note)

OPTIONAL TOPPING

Vegan vanilla ice cream

If using the vegan butter, slice it into cubes. Then place it in the freezer to firm up and chill. If using the coconut oil, measure it in a cup and place in the refrigerator to solidify. Take it out, slice it into small cubes and then place it back in the refrigerator until you get the other crust ingredients ready.

Sift the flour with the cinnamon, salt and sugar and mix together with a whisk. Set it aside.

Prepare the ice water, adding some ice cubes to a glass of room-temperature water. Let it sit for a few minutes so the ice melts and chills the water.

Using a pastry cutter or two knives, cut the coconut oil or butter cubes into the flour mixture, until the pieces of solid oil or butter are about the size of peas. Use your fingers to quickly crumble everything together. Sprinkle 3 tablespoons (45 ml) of ice water over the dough, and gently knead it with your hands. Add more ice water as needed, just a tablespoon (15 ml) at a time, until the dough comes together when you squeeze it, and you can form a ball that doesn't crumble. Work the pastry very briefly, just to get it to stick together as a dough. The dough shouldn't be wet or too sticky. If the dough seems wet, add a little more flour into the mix. If the dough is not holding together or appears crumbly, add a little bit more ice water.

Shape the dough into a disc, wrap it in plastic wrap and refrigerate for 30 minutes. Once the dough has chilled, arrange a rack in the middle of the oven and preheat the oven to 375°F (190°C) on conventional-baking mode.

To prepare the filling, place the blackberries into a small bowl. Sprinkle them with the tapioca starch, ½ teaspoon of cinnamon and syrup. Set aside. When you add the filling to the galette, do not include any of the liquid juices because they could make the bottom soggy; use a slotted spoon to avoid the liquid.

(continued)

NOTE: The amount of sweetener used in the filling is adjustable and depends on how sweet your berries and fruits are and how sweet you'd like the galette to be. The amount I included would be medium-sweet. To achieve an even sweeter taste, increase the amount of sweetener by 2 tablespoons (20 g). Add 1 tablespoon (10 g) of coconut sugar to each fruit, so 2 tablespoons (20 g) total.

Take out the chilled dough and let it sit at room temperature for about 10 minutes to become more pliable, then unwrap it and place it on a piece of floured parchment paper. Sprinkle some flour on top of the dough and cover it with another piece of paper. Using a rolling pin, roll out the pastry into a rectangular shape. You should get a 10 x 14–inch (25 x 36–cm) rectangle. The pastry should be 1 inch (2.5 cm) thick. If the dough sticks to the paper, add a little bit more flour and keep rolling. When you're done, slide the parchment paper with the rolled-out pastry onto a large baking sheet and discard the top paper.

Sprinkle the tapioca starch over the dough and arrange the blackberry filling on top of it, leaving a 1½- to 2-inch (4- to 5-cm) border around the edge. Next, neatly assemble the peach slices over the blackberry layer so the slices overlap. When done, sprinkle them with the remaining ½ teaspoon of cinnamon and 2 tablespoons (20 g) of coconut sugar. Use the parchment paper to fold the dough over the edges of the fruit, and press gently where the pastry folds over to ensure the fruit gets tucked into the dough. A large part of the filling shall remain uncovered.

Sprinkle the remaining 1 tablespoon (10 g) of sugar over the whole galette for more crunchiness and sweetness.

Bake on conventional-baking mode for 15 minutes, then another 15 minutes on fan-assisted mode to get a nice crunchy crust. It is done when the filling is bubbly and the crust is nicely browned and feels sturdy when you tap on it. If you're baking it only on conventional-baking mode, prolong the baking to 35 minutes, or until the crust has that nice golden-brown color around the edges.

Leave the galette to cool down for about 20 to 30 minutes before slicing so it can firm up. Serve the galette warm, and add vegan ice cream, if using, for even more deliciousness. It will keep for up to 3 days in the refrigerator and for up to 2 days at room temperature.

CHOCOLATE RASPBERRY GALETTE

GLUTEN FREE; NUT FREE | YIELD: 6–8 SLICES

Why is chocolate pastry galette not a thing? I think it totally should be, because guys, this chocolate raspberry galette tastes freaking amazing! You should know by now that chocolate with raspberries is one of my favorite combinations of flavors—the tartness of raspberries goes perfectly with the sweet, bitter and heavy taste of dark chocolate. I thought I should make it double chocolate by adding not only unsweetened cocoa to the crust but also chopped dark chocolate on top of it. I think you're gonna love it!

CRUST

½ cup (120 ml) melted extra virgin coconut oil

⅔ cup (95 g) buckwheat flour

½ cup (70 g) brown rice flour

2 tbsp (20 g) coconut sugar

⅓ tsp salt

1 tbsp (10 g) tapioca starch

3 tbsp (30 g) unsweetened cocoa powder

4 tbsp (60 ml) ice water

FILLING

2½ cups (325 g) raspberries

¼ cup plus 1 tbsp (43 g) coconut sugar, divided (see Notes)

1 tbsp (10 g) tapioca starch

1 tsp vanilla powder or 2 tsp (10 ml) vanilla extract

½ cup (90 g) chopped dark vegan chocolate

Measure the coconut oil in a cup and place it in the refrigerator for at least 2 to 3 hours to solidify. Then take it out, slice it into small cubes and place it back in the refrigerator while you get the other crust ingredients ready.

Sift the flours with the sugar, salt, tapioca starch and cocoa powder. Mix using a whisk. Prepare ice water by adding some ice cubes to tap water and letting them completely melt.

Using a pastry cutter or two knives, cut the coconut oil cubes into the flour mixture until the pieces of solid oil are about the size of peas. Use your fingers to quickly crumble everything together. Sprinkle 3 tablespoons (45 ml) of ice water over the dough mixture, gently kneading the dough with your hands. Add more of the ice water as needed, just 1 tablespoon (15 ml) at a time, until the dough comes together when you squeeze it, and you can form a ball that doesn't crumble. Work on the pastry very briefly, just to get it to stick in a dough. The dough shouldn't be wet or too sticky. If it seems wet, add a little more flour. If the dough is not holding together or appears crumbly, add a little bit more ice water.

Shape the dough into a disc, wrap it in plastic wrap and refrigerate for 30 minutes. Once the dough has chilled, arrange a rack in the middle of the oven and preheat the oven to 375°F (190°C) on conventional-baking mode.

To prepare the filling, place the raspberries in a bowl and sprinkle them with ¼ cup (33 g) of sugar, tapioca starch and vanilla. Gently mix. When you add the filling to the galette, do not include any of the liquid juices because they could make the bottom soggy.

(continued)

NOTES: The raspberry filling will not be overly sweet, but I think it complements the chocolate nicely. However, if you want the recipe to be sweeter, feel free to increase the amount of coconut sugar by 1 or 2 tablespoons (10 to 20 g).

You can use unbleached all-purpose flour for this crust, but I do encourage you to try these alternative flours because they give a different and very delicious taste to the galette as well as add much more nutritional value.

Take out the chilled dough and let it sit at room temperature for about 10 minutes to become more pliable, then unwrap it and place it on floured parchment paper. Sprinkle some flour on top of the dough and cover it with another piece of paper. Using a rolling pin, roll out the pastry into a rectangular shape. You should get a 10 x 14–inch (25 x 36–cm) rectangle. The pastry should be 1 inch (2.5 cm) thick. If the dough sticks to the paper, add a little bit more flour and keep rolling. When you're done, slide the parchment paper with the rolled-out pastry onto a large baking sheet and discard the top paper.

Once the pastry is ready, toss the chopped chocolate on the rolled-out pastry leaving about a 1½- to 2-inch (4- to 5-cm) border around the edge. Assemble the prepared raspberries on top of it. Lifting the parchment paper, use it to gently fold the edges of the dough over the fruit filling, pressing gently to ensure that the fruit gets tucked into the dough. A large part of the filling will remain uncovered. Sprinkle the remaining 1 tablespoon (10 g) sugar over the whole galette.

Bake it on conventional-baking mode for 15 minutes, then another 15 minutes on fan-assisted mode to get a crunchy crust. It is done when the filling is nice and bubbly and the crust feels sturdy when you tap on it. If you're baking it only on conventional-baking mode, prolong the baking to 35 minutes, or until the crust has that nice golden-brown color around the edges.

Remove the galette from the oven and leave it to cool down for about 20 to 30 minutes before slicing. It is best eaten freshly baked. It will keep in the refrigerator for up to 3 days or for up to 2 days at room temperature.

BUCKWHEAT CRUST STRAWBERRY GALETTE

GLUTEN FREE; NUT FREE | YIELD: 6 SLICES

I have to say that buckwheat pie crust is my favorite for its delicious, crunchy texture and beautiful strong flavor. When used in combination with some of my favorite summer berries, it is quite a flavor explosion. This is one of the recipes that makes me wait impatiently for strawberry season every single year.

CRUST

½ cup (112 g) vegan butter or ½ cup (120 ml) melted extra virgin coconut oil

1¼ cups (165 g) buckwheat flour

2 tbsp (20 g) tapioca starch

⅓ tsp salt

2 tbsp (20 g) coconut sugar

½ tsp vanilla powder

4 to 5 tbsp (60 to 75 ml) ice cold water

FILLING

2½ cups (340 g) strawberries

½ tsp vanilla powder

Pinch of ground ginger

3 tbsp (45 ml) maple syrup

1 tbsp (15 ml) lemon juice

2 tbsp (20 g) coconut sugar, divided (see Note)

1½ tbsp (15 g) tapioca starch

OPTIONAL TOPPING

Vegan vanilla ice cream

If using the vegan butter, slice it into cubes. Then place it in the freezer to firm up and chill. If using the coconut oil, measure it in a cup, and place it in the refrigerator to solidify. Then take it out, slice it into small cubes and place it back in the refrigerator while you get the other crust ingredients ready.

Sift the flour with the tapioca, salt, sugar and vanilla and mix together using a whisk.

Prepare the ice water by adding some water and ice cubes to a glass. Set it aside to melt.

Using a pastry cutter or two knives, cut the coconut oil cubes or butter into the flour mixture until the pieces are about the size of peas. Use your fingers to quickly crumble everything together. Sprinkle 3 tablespoons (45 ml) of ice water over the dough mixture, gently kneading the dough with your hands. Add more of the ice water as needed, just 1 tablespoon (15 ml) at a time, until the dough comes together when you squeeze it, and you can form a ball that doesn't crumble. Work on the pastry very briefly, just to get it to stick in a dough. The dough shouldn't be wet or too sticky. If the dough seems wet, add a little more flour into the mix. If the dough is not holding together or appears crumbly, add a little bit more ice water.

Shape the dough into a disc, wrap it in plastic wrap and refrigerate for 30 minutes. Once the dough has chilled, arrange a rack in the middle of the oven and preheat the oven to 375°F (190°C) on conventional-baking mode.

To prepare the filling, place the strawberries in a bowl and add the vanilla, ginger, syrup, lemon juice and 1 tablespoon (10 g) of sugar. Mix to cover the fruits and then sprinkle with the tapioca starch. Gently mix until the berries are coated. The fruits will release some liquid, so be careful to not include any of the juice when adding the filling to the galette, because it will make the bottom of the pastry soggy.

(continued)

NOTE: The amount of sweetener used in the filling is adjustable and depends on how sweet your berries are and how sweet you'd like the galette to be. The amount I included would be medium-sweet. To achieve an even sweeter taste, increase the amount of sweetener by 1 tablespoon (10 g).

Take out the chilled dough and let it sit at room temperature for about 10 minutes to become more pliable, then unwrap it and place it on floured parchment paper. Sprinkle some flour on top of the dough and cover it with another piece of paper. Using a rolling pin, roll out the pastry into a circular shape. The pastry should be 1 inch (2.5 cm) thick. If the dough sticks to the paper, add a little bit more flour and keep rolling. When you're done, slide the parchment paper with the rolled-out pastry onto a large baking sheet and discard the top paper.

Arrange the filling over the rolled-out dough, leaving a 1½- to 2-inch (4- to 5-cm) border around the edge. Lifting the parchment paper, use it to fold the edges of the dough over the fruit filling, pressing gently to ensure that the fruit gets tucked into the dough. A large part of the filling will remain uncovered.

Sprinkle the remaining 1 tablespoon (10 g) of sugar over the whole galette, especially over the pastry for an even crunchier crust.

Bake on conventional-baking mode for 15 minutes, then another 15 minutes on fan-assisted mode to get a crunchy crust. It is done when the filling is bubbly and the crust is nicely browned and feels sturdy when you tap on it. If you're baking it only on conventional-baking mode, prolong the baking to 35 minutes, or until the crust has that nice golden-brown color around the edges.

Leave it to cool down for about 20 to 30 minutes before slicing. It is best eaten freshly baked while it is still warm. Serve it with a scoop of vegan ice cream, if using, for even more deliciousness. It will keep in the refrigerator for up to 3 days or for up to 2 days at room temperature.

BLACKBERRY *and* RASPBERRY GALETTE

GLUTEN FREE | YIELD: 6–8 SLICES

This galette is a perfect light dessert. The combination of the juiciness of gorgeous fresh berries, delicious crunchy rice and almond flour crust will awaken your senses and satisfy your sweet cravings, while you're actually just enjoying a bunch of fruits with some nutritious and wholesome add-ons. Cool, right?

CRUST

½ cup (120 ml) melted extra virgin coconut oil

4 to 5 tbsp (60 to 75 ml) ice water

¾ cup (110 g) brown rice flour

½ cup (60 g) almond flour

1 tbsp (10 g) coconut sugar

½ tsp xanthan gum

⅓ tsp salt

½ tsp vanilla powder

FILLING

1 cup (130 g) raspberries

2½ cups (300 g) blackberries

2 tbsp (20 g) tapioca starch, divided

¼ tsp cinnamon

¼ tsp vanilla

4 tbsp (60 ml) agave syrup, divided

1 tbsp (10 g) coconut sugar

Measure the coconut oil in a cup and place it in the refrigerator for at least 2 hours to solidify. Then take it out, slice it into small cubes and place it back in the refrigerator while you get the other crust ingredients ready.

Prepare the ice water by adding some ice cubes to tap water and let them melt and chill the water for 5 minutes.

Sift the flours with the sugar, xanthan gum, salt and vanilla powder and mix well using a whisk.

Using a pastry cutter or two knives, cut the coconut oil cubes into the flour mixture until the pieces of solid oil are about the size of peas. Use your fingers to quickly crumble everything together. Sprinkle 3 tablespoons (45 ml) of ice water over the dough mixture, gently kneading the dough with your hands. Add more of the ice water as needed, just 1 tablespoon (15 ml) at a time, until the dough comes together when you squeeze it, and you can form a ball that doesn't crumble. Work on the pastry very briefly, just to get it to stick in a dough. The dough shouldn't be wet or too sticky. If the dough seems wet, add a little more rice flour into the mix. If the dough is not holding together or appears crumbly, add a little bit more ice water.

Shape the dough into a disc, wrap it in plastic wrap and refrigerate for 30 minutes. Once the dough has chilled, arrange a rack in the middle of the oven and preheat the oven to 375°F (190°C) on conventional-baking mode.

To prepare the filling, place raspberries in one bowl and blackberries in another. Add 1½ tablespoons (15 g) of tapioca starch, the cinnamon, vanilla and 2 table-spoons (30 ml) of syrup to the blackberries and ½ teaspoon of tapioca starch and 2 tablespoons (30 ml) of syrup to the raspberries. When you add the filling to the galette, do not include any of the liquid juices, because they could make the bottom of the pastry soggy.

(continued)

NOTE:
The amount of sweetener used in the filling is adjustable and depends on how sweet your berries and fruits are and how sweet you'd like the galette to be. The amount I included would be medium-sweet. To achieve an even sweeter taste, increase the amount of sweetener by 2 tablespoons (20 g). Add 1 tablespoon (10 g) of coconut sugar to each fruit, so 2 tablespoons (20 g) total.

Take out the chilled dough and let it sit at room temperature for about 10 minutes to become more pliable, then unwrap it and place it on floured parchment paper. Sprinkle some flour on top of the dough and cover it with another piece of paper. Using a rolling pin, roll out the pastry into a rectangular shape. You should get a 10 x 14–inch (25 x 36–cm) rectangle. The pastry should be 1 inch (2.5 cm) thick. If the dough sticks to the paper, add a little bit more flour and keep rolling. When you're done, slide the parchment paper with the rolled-out pastry onto a large baking sheet and discard the top paper.

Next, place the prepared fruits on the pastry leaving around a 1½- to 2-inch (4- to 5-cm) border around the edge. Fold the edges of the parchment paper over the filling, and use it to gently fold the edges of the dough over the fruit filling, pressing gently to ensure that the fruit gets tucked into the dough. A large part of the filling will remain uncovered.

Sprinkle the coconut sugar over the whole galette, especially the pastry for more crunchiness. Place it in the preheated oven and bake on conventional-baking mode for 15 minutes, then another 15 minutes on fan-assisted mode to get a crunchy crust. It is done when the filling is bubbly and the crust is browned and feels sturdy when you tap on it. If you're baking it only on conventional-baking mode, prolong the baking to 35 minutes, or until the crust has that nice golden-brown color around the edges.

Remove from the oven and leave the galette to cool for about 20 to 30 minutes before slicing. It is best eaten freshly baked. Serve it with some vegan ice cream for even more deliciousness. It will keep in the refrigerator for up to 3 days or for 2 days at room temperature.

APPLE ALMOND GALETTE

GLUTEN FREE | YIELD: 10–12 SLICES

In this recipe, I started out trying to make a gluten-free apple pie, but I failed miserably. First, I ambitiously tried making a gluten-free crust out of several different kinds of flours, then I had to give up after my second or third attempt because it kept falling apart. Finally, upset over the wasted ingredients, I settled for remaking them into a galette—and the result turned out even better than a pie! This apple almond galette with gluten-free crust is out-of-this-world amazing! It features a crunchy, fragrant and delicious crust with juicy caramelized apples and almonds in the center. So good! Once more, a failure turned into a success . . . and with this recipe, hopefully you'll realize, like I did, that sometimes sticking to simple and delicious is the way to go when it comes to vegan baking.

CRUST

⅔ cup (150 g) cold vegan butter or ⅔ cup (160 ml) melted extra virgin coconut oil

7 to 8 tbsp (105 to 120 ml) ice water

1 cup plus 3 tbsp (185 g) brown rice flour

1 cup (140 g) buckwheat flour

3 tbsp (30 g) coconut sugar

1 tsp xanthan gum

1 tsp cinnamon

½ tsp fine salt

FILLING

6 cups (700 g) thinly sliced, peeled apples

1 tbsp (15 ml) lemon juice

⅔ cup (95 g) coconut sugar

1½ tsp (4 g) cinnamon

⅓ tsp fine sea salt

2 tbsp (20 g) tapioca starch

If using the vegan butter, slice it into cubes. Then place it in the freezer to firm up and chill. If using coconut oil, measure it in a cup and place it in the refrigerator to solidify. Then take it out, slice it into small cubes and place it back in the refrigerator until you get the other crust ingredients ready.

Fill a glass with water and add ice cubes. Set it aside to melt.

To prepare the crust, sift the flours, sugar, xanthan gum, cinnamon and salt into a large mixing bowl. Mix with a whisk and add the chilled vegan butter or coconut oil. Using a pastry cutter or two knives, cut the butter or oil into the flour mixture, until the pieces are about the size of peas. Then use your fingers to quickly crumble everything together. Sprinkle 6 tablespoons (90 ml) of ice water over the dough mixture; gently knead the dough with your hands. Add more of the ice water as needed, just 1 tablespoon (15 ml) at a time, until the dough comes together when you squeeze it, and you can form a ball that doesn't crumble. The dough shouldn't be wet or too sticky. If the dough seems wet, add a little more flour into the mix. If the dough is not holding together or appears crumbly, add a little bit more ice water.

Shape the dough into a disc, wrap it in plastic wrap and refrigerate it for 30 minutes. Once the dough has chilled, arrange a rack in the middle of the oven and preheat the oven to 375°F (190°C) on conventional-baking mode.

To make the filling, add the apples to a bowl and gently season them with the lemon juice, sugar, cinnamon and salt. Mix together and sprinkle it with tapioca starch. Gently mix again until the apple slices are coated in seasonings. The apples will release some juices, so when you add the filling to the galette, be careful not to include any liquid as it will make the bottom of the pastry soggy.

(continued)

½ tbsp (8 ml) maple syrup

½ tbsp (8 ml) plant milk

2 tbsp (20 g) flaked slivered almonds

1 to 2 tsp (5 to 10 g) coconut sugar for sprinkling

OPTIONAL TOPPING

Vegan vanilla ice cream

Bring the dough to room temperature for 10 minutes to make it pliable enough to roll. Unwrap it and place it on a large floured piece of parchment paper. Sift a small amount of flour on top of it and cover with a second piece of paper. Using a rolling pin, roll the dough into a 20-inch (50-cm) round shape that is around 1 inch (2.5 cm) thick. If the dough sticks to the paper, add a little bit more flour. When you're done rolling, slide the parchment paper with the dough onto a large baking sheet and discard the top paper.

Arrange the filling over the rolled-out dough, leaving a 1½- to 2-inch (4- to 5-cm) border around the edge. Fold the edges of the dough up over the filling to form a crust, ensuring the fruit gets tucked into the dough. A large part of the filling will remain uncovered.

Prepare the brushing mixture by whisking together syrup and milk. Brush the tops and edges of the dough. Sprinkle with flaked almonds, press them gently onto the crust and filling, then sprinkle the galette with more sugar, making sure to get some on the pastry for even more crunchiness.

Bake in your preheated oven for 30 minutes until the apple slices and almonds have nice golden edges and the crust is deeply golden brown and sturdy when you tap it.

I recommend baking it for 15 minutes on conventional-baking mode then for another 15 minutes on fan-assisted mode to get a nicer color and more crunchiness to the crust. If you're baking it only on conventional-baking mode, prolong the baking to 35 minutes, or until the crust has that nice golden-brown color around the edges.

Transfer the galette to cool on a wire rack and serve warm. Serve it with vegan vanilla ice cream, if using, for even more deliciousness.

NOTE: For this pastry, you can use either well-chilled vegan butter or coconut oil. It is a tad more difficult to work with coconut oil, but it gives such an amazing crunchiness and flavor to the pastry that I think it makes it really worthwhile, so I encourage you to go for it. Also, coconut oil is a much more wholesome ingredient compared to vegan butter.

STRAWBERRY ALMOND CRUMBLE

GLUTEN FREE | YIELD: 1 (7-INCH [18-CM]) CRUMBLE; 4-6 SERVINGS

Summer fruits and berries are just perfect for making crumbles because they are soft and juicy
and bake in the same amount of time the streusel topping does. You can prep this dish in just ten minutes
and bake it in just thirty minutes. This delicious crumble is best served warm as a sweet treat
after dinner, with tea or even for breakfast.

---

3 cups (400 g) strawberries (see Notes)

2 tbsp (20 g) coconut sugar

1 tbsp (15 ml) maple syrup

¼ tsp vanilla powder or ½ tsp vanilla extract

1 tbsp (10 g) tapioca starch

2 pinches of Himalayan salt

1½ tsp (7 ml) lemon juice

CRUMBLE TOPPING

½ cup (70 g) brown rice flour (see Notes)

½ cup (50 g) old fashioned rolled oats (see Notes)

1 cup (85 g) flaked almonds

½ tsp vanilla powder

¼ tsp fine Himalayan salt

¼ cup (60 ml) maple syrup (see Notes)

⅓ cup (80 ml) melted extra virgin coconut oil

2 tbsp (30 ml) lemon juice

OPTIONAL TOPPINGS

Vegan vanilla ice cream

Vegan Greek yogurt

Fresh strawberries

Preheat the oven to 375°F (190°C).

Place the strawberries in a large bowl and add the sugar, syrup, vanilla, tapioca starch, salt and lemon juice. Stir to coat the berries.

To make the crumble topping, place the flour, oats, almonds, vanilla, salt, syrup, oil and lemon juice in a medium-sized mixing bowl. Mix everything with your clean hands until the mixture is moist and crumbly.

Transfer the strawberry mixture to a 7-inch (18-cm) square baking dish, level it and toss the crumble on top. Bake in the oven for about 30 to 35 minutes or until the topping is slightly golden brown and the fruits are bubbling. Enjoy it warm, and serve with some vegan vanilla ice cream or vegan Greek yogurt and more strawberries, if using.

You can store leftovers in the refrigerator for 4 to 5 days. You can also freeze the crumble in an airtight container for up to 3 months. To serve, let it thaw to room temperature, then reheat in the oven for 5 to 10 minutes.

NOTES: Feel free to make this crumble using any other berries. Just stick to the amount listed in the ingredient list.

You can use fresh or frozen berries. When using frozen berries, increase the amount of starch to 2 tablespoons (20 g), because the berries will release more liquid when baking.

You can substitute rice flour with any other flour of choice.

To ensure the recipe is gluten free, be sure to use certified gluten-free oats.

You can substitute the maple syrup in the crumble topping for a combination of 3 tablespoons (30 g) of coconut sugar and 2 tablespoons (30 ml) of maple syrup, as coconut sugar will give a bit more crunchiness to the topping.

ONE-BOWL APPLE BREAKFAST CRUMBLE

GLUTEN FREE | YIELD: 1 (8-INCH [20-CM]) CRUMBLE; 4-6 SERVINGS

This super simple, one-bowl recipe will make a beautiful breakfast or dessert that is bursting with flavors but is also full of goodness. This is almost an apple granola as far as the ingredients list is concerned—it mostly uses fruits, oats, nuts and natural sweeteners. Serve it as a rich decadent dessert with a dollop of vegan vanilla ice cream, as a delicious and nourishing breakfast as it is or with some vegan Greek yogurt.

FILLING

2 tbsp (30 ml) melted extra virgin coconut oil

¼ cup (33 g) coconut sugar

1 tsp vanilla powder or 2 tsp (10 ml) vanilla extract

2 pinches of Himalayan salt

1 tbsp (15 ml) lemon juice

1 tsp cinnamon

Pinch of ground ginger

1 tsp tapioca starch

3½ cups (400 g) diced apples, ½-inch (1.3-cm) cubes

TOPPING

1 cup (100 g) old fashioned rolled oats, divided (see Notes)

¼ cup (30 g) chopped walnuts

1 tsp vanilla powder or 2 tsp (10 ml) vanilla extract

½ tsp cinnamon

2 pinches of Himalayan salt

⅛ tsp baking powder

1 tbsp (10 g) coconut sugar

2 tbsp (30 ml) maple syrup

3 tbsp (45 ml) melted coconut oil

1 tsp lemon juice

OPTIONAL

Vegan vanilla ice cream

Vegan Greek yogurt

Preheat the oven to 355°F (180°C). Prepare an 8-inch (20-cm) square baking dish or a rectangular dish of a similar volume. If desired, grease the dish with coconut oil.

Whisk oil with the sugar, vanilla, salt, lemon juice, cinnamon, ginger and tapioca starch. Add the apples and toss so the apples are nicely covered. Transfer them to the baking dish and level with a spoon.

To make the topping, measure ½ cup (50 g) of oats and grind them into flour using a food processor or coffee grinder. Add them to the same bowl you used for apples and add the rest of the topping ingredients: the remaining oats, chopped walnuts, vanilla, cinnamon, salt, baking powder, sugar, syrup, oil and lemon juice. Mix everything with clean hands until the mixture is moist and crumbly. Add the crumble topping to the baking dish, spreading it evenly over the fruits, using a spoon to cover them. I like leaving ½ inch (1.3 cm) of fruits uncovered around the edges to see the bubbling fruits during baking.

Bake in the oven for about 30 to 35 minutes or until the crumble topping is golden brown and the fruits are bubbling.

Enjoy warm and serve with some vegan vanilla ice cream or vegan Greek yogurt, if using.

Store leftovers in a sealed container at room temperature for up to 2 days. Store refrigerated for up to 5 days. You can also freeze the crumble in an airtight container for up to 3 months. To serve, let the crumble thaw to room temperature, then reheat in the oven for 5 to 10 minutes.

NOTES: This recipe is pretty flexible, and you can play around with the fruit-to-crumble-topping ratio. I went for a more fruity experience in this recipe, but feel free to double the topping ingredients.

Same as in all other crumbles, I recommend using old-fashioned rolled oats and not quick oats because they work better in the crumble topping and will not get mushy.

To ensure this recipe is gluten free, be sure to use certified gluten-free oats.

BLUEBERRY PLUM CRUMBLE

GLUTEN FREE | YIELD: 1 (8-INCH [20-CM]) CRUMBLE; 4-6 SERVINGS

I especially love plums in baking. It's interesting how such modest fresh fruits become incredibly rich tasting and flavorful in baking, especially when enhanced with spices like cinnamon, ginger and vanilla. These beautifully soft, juicy and almost creamy fruits act as a contrast to a crunchy golden topping; this crumble is bursting with flavors of fruits, vanilla and spices. On top of it, it is such an easy, fuss-free recipe. Once you try it, you might be in danger of making it on repeat.

FILLING

2 cups (280 g) pitted plums, cut in half or quarters

2 cups (300 g) blueberries

¼ cup (33 g) coconut sugar

¼ tsp vanilla powder or ½ tsp vanilla extract

1 tbsp (10 g) tapioca starch

Pinch of Himalayan salt

1 tsp lemon juice

½ tsp cinnamon

Pinch of ground ginger

TOPPING

2 tbsp (20 g) almond flour (see Notes)

1 cup (100 g) old fashioned rolled oats (see Notes)

½ tsp vanilla powder or 1 tsp vanilla extract

½ tsp cinnamon

2 pinches of Himalayan salt

2 tbsp (30 ml) maple syrup

3 tbsp (45 ml) melted extra virgin coconut oil

½ tbsp (8 ml) lemon juice

OPTIONAL TOPPINGS

Vegan vanilla ice cream

Vegan Greek yogurt

Fresh berries

Preheat the oven to 355°F (180°C).

Add the sliced plums and the blueberries to a large bowl and add the sugar, vanilla, tapioca starch, salt, lemon juice, cinnamon and ginger. Mix to combine.

To make the topping, place the flour, oats, vanilla, cinnamon, salt, syrup, oil and lemon juice in a medium-sized mixing bowl. Mix everything with clean hands until the mixture is moist and crumbly.

Transfer the fruit mixture to an 8-inch (20-cm) square pan, level it and add the crumble topping on top.

Bake in the oven for about 30 to 35 minutes or until the crumble topping is golden brown and the fruits are bubbling. Enjoy the crumble warm. Serve with some vegan vanilla ice cream or vegan Greek yogurt and more fresh berries, if using.

Store leftovers in the refrigerator for up to 4 to 5 days. You can also freeze the crumble in an airtight container for up to 3 months. To serve, let it thaw at room temperature, then reheat it in the oven for 5 to 10 minutes.

NOTES: I recommend using rolled oats and not quick oats because they work better in the crumble topping—they will not get mushy.

To ensure the crumble is gluten free, be sure to use certified gluten-free oats in the recipe.

Feel free to make this crumble using just plums, or peaches or any other soft fruits, really. Just stick to the amount of fruits used.

To make this crumble outside plum season, you can slice plums in half, remove the pit and freeze the slices in plastic bags.

You can substitute almond flour with any other flour of choice.

CHOCOLATE SPIKED PLUM CRUMBLE

GLUTEN FREE | YIELD: 1 (9 X 7-INCH [23 X 18-CM]) CRUMBLE; 6 SERVINGS

Why is making chocolate fruit crumbles not a thing? I have no idea, but I decided to try making one—oh, what a success! Imagine soft fragrant plums bursting with the aroma of fruit, vanilla and rum, all of it underneath a crumbly chocolate topping with melted chocolate chunks. Do I have your attention?

FILLING

5 cups (500 g) pitted and quartered plums

1 tbsp (15 ml) vanilla extract or 1 tsp vanilla powder

2 tsp (10 ml) dark rum

Small pinch of salt

¼ cup (33 g) coconut sugar

1 tbsp (10 g) tapioca starch

1 tbsp (15 ml) agave syrup

1 tbsp (15 ml) lemon juice

TOPPING

1½ cups (150 g) old fashioned rolled oats (see Notes)

½ cup (50 g) almond flour (see Notes)

1 tsp vanilla extract or ½ tsp vanilla powder

⅓ cup (80 ml) melted extra virgin coconut oil

4 tbsp (60 ml) agave or maple syrup

2 pinches of fine Himalayan salt

3 tbsp (30 g) unsweetened cocoa powder

⅓ cup (65 g) chopped vegan dark chocolate or vegan chocolate chips

Vegan vanilla ice cream, optional

Preheat the oven to 350°F (175°C).

Add the sliced plums to a large bowl, then add the vanilla, rum, salt, sugar, tapioca starch, syrup and lemon juice. Mix to coat the plums.

To make the topping, place the oats, flour, vanilla, oil, syrup, salt, cocoa powder and chocolate in a medium-sized mixing bowl. Mix everything with your hands until the mixture is evenly moist and crumbly.

Transfer the fruit mixture to a 9 x 7–inch (23 x 18–cm) baking dish (or a dish of similar size), level it and add the crumble on top.

Bake in the oven for about 30 minutes or until the crumble is crunchy and the fruits are bubbling.

Enjoy the crumble warm. It is best served with some vegan vanilla ice cream.

You can store the leftovers in the refrigerator for up to 4 to 5 days. Freeze in an airtight container for up to 3 months. Before serving, let it thaw to room temperature, then reheat in the oven for 5 to 10 minutes.

NOTES: You can make this crumble with your favorite fruit and chocolate combination, as long as you use a soft fruit and keep the ratios. Feel free to substitute almond flour with any grain flour of choice—like all-purpose, brown rice, oat, buckwheat or white spelt. They will all work.

To ensure the crumble is gluten free, be sure to use certified gluten-free oats in the recipe.

BREAKFAST BAKES AND BITE-SIZED TREATS

This chapter is all about simple, everyday treats that aren't even necessarily desserts but can be nutritious and wholesome breakfasts, snacks or even pre- or post-workout energy bites. Whether you're after a delicious sweet breakfast or a quick bite to satisfy the sweet cravings, totally guilt free, this chapter is for you.

Why not have your home basking in the divine smell of cinnamon and pancakes or waffles in the morning while you enjoy dessert for breakfast? Some of my favorites include The Fluffiest Blueberry Chia Pancakes (page 119), which I love having smothered in coconut yogurt and fresh berries or even incredibly rich but healthy Homemade Nutella (page 119) for a super decadent treat, and the gorgeously Crunchy Buckwheat Waffles (page 123) that are so easy, fuss free and delicious. And don't forget the small bites that I like having when I feel a bit hungry between meals or am just a little peckish, like Buckwheat Hazelnut and Chocolate Bliss Balls (page 131) or Walnut and Caramel Chocolate Bars (page 132).

CHOCOLATE CHIP WALNUT BANANA BREAD

YIELD: 1 (9 X 5-INCH [23 X 13-CM]) LOAF

This is the best way to use up overripe bananas! This fluffy and soft banana bread will delight you with the delicious flavors and fragrance of bananas, vanilla and walnuts. It's a sweet nutritious breakfast, but it also works out wonderfully as a dessert. Enjoy it by itself or with a drizzle of Homemade Dark Chocolate Coating (page 74), nut butter and fruits.

½ cup (80 g) almonds

½ cup (65 g) white spelt flour

1 tsp baking powder

½ tsp baking soda

⅓ tsp Himalayan salt

1 tsp vanilla powder or 2 tsp (10 ml) vanilla extract

1 tbsp (15 g) golden flax seeds

3 tbsp (45 ml) water

3 very ripe bananas, peeled, plus 1 banana for decoration, divided

⅓ cup (80 ml) melted extra virgin coconut oil

⅓ cup (44 g) plus ½ tsp coconut sugar, divided

2 tbsp (30 ml) lemon juice

1 tsp apple cider vinegar

½ cup (55 g) walnuts

⅓ cup (65 g) vegan chocolate chips or chopped dark vegan chocolate, divided

OPTIONAL TOPPINGS

Homemade Dark Chocolate Coating (page 74)

Homemade Nutella (page 119)

Nut butter of choice

Fresh berries and fruits

Preheat the oven to 350°F (175°C). Arrange a rack in the bottom third of the oven. Line a 9 x 5-inch (23 x 13–cm) loaf pan with parchment paper, letting the excess hang over the sides.

Grind the almonds in a food processor and set them aside. In a large mixing bowl, sift the flour with the baking powder, baking soda, salt and vanilla. Add the ground almonds and mix with a whisk to combine.

Grind the flax seeds for a flax egg using a coffee grinder or a small food processor and place them in a small bowl. Add the water and mix, leaving it to thicken.

In the food processor, blend 3 bananas with the oil, ⅓ cup (44 g) of the sugar, lemon juice and vinegar.

Add the banana mixture and flax egg to the dry ingredients. Gently fold, using a silicone spatula or a large wooden spoon, until the ingredients are just barely combined. Do not overmix; it's okay if you can see a few traces of flour.

Chop the walnuts and fold them into the batter along with the chocolate chips, reserving a few pieces of chocolate to decorate the bread.

Pour the batter into the prepared loaf pan and smooth out the top of the batter using a spatula or a spoon. Slice the remaining banana in half lengthwise and sprinkle with the remaining sugar. Arrange the halves on top of the batter, sugared side up, and press very gently into the batter. Scatter the reserved pieces of chocolate and press them in gently.

Bake the bread in the preheated oven for 45 minutes on fan-assisted mode or in a conventional oven for 1 hour, or until a toothpick inserted into the center comes out mostly clean or with just a few moist crumbs attached. Transfer the pan onto a wire rack and cool for 10 to 15 minutes, then remove the bread from the baking pan. Slide the knife along the not-lined sides. Pulling by the excess part of parchment paper, take it gently out of the pan and place it on the rack to cool down completely. Cut into slices and serve as it is, or for an even more indulgent treat, top it with homemade chocolate or nut butter of choice and fresh berries.

Store it in an airtight container or wrap it tightly in the plastic wrap, and leave it on the countertop for up to 4 days. Refrigerate for up to 1 week. You can also freeze the banana bread for up to 3 months. Allow it to defrost on the countertop before serving.

THE FLUFFIEST BLUEBERRY CHIA PANCAKES
and HOMEMADE NUTELLA

YIELD: 10 PANCAKES

Light and fluffy, just a little browned around the edges and loaded with fresh juicy blueberries, these yummy pancakes have become a staple in my home. Drizzle them with Homemade Nutella for a dreamy and indulgent but nourishing breakfast. Every kid loves Nutella, and probably every grown-up does as well, so these just might become your favorite sweet breakfast too.

HOMEMADE NUTELLA

1½ cups (210 g) hazelnuts

2 tbsp (30 ml) melted extra virgin coconut oil

4 tbsp (60 ml) maple syrup

4 to 5 tbsp (40 to 50 g) unsweetened cocoa powder

½ cup (120 ml) water plus 2 tbsp (30 ml) if you want your Nutella less thick and more spreadable

Tiny pinch of salt

PANCAKES

1 cup (240 ml) oat milk, room temperature

1 tbsp (15 ml) lemon juice

1½ cups (185 g) white spelt flour, plus more to coat blueberries

2 tsp (7 g) baking powder

2 tbsp (20 g) coconut sugar

⅓ tsp Himalayan salt

1 tsp vanilla extract or ½ tsp vanilla powder, optional

1 tbsp (12 g) chia seeds

1 tbsp (15 ml) melted extra virgin coconut oil, plus about ½ tsp for each pancake to cook

1 cup (135 g) cup fresh or frozen blueberries

Fresh berries, to serve

To make the Homemade Nutella, roast the hazelnuts on 300°F (150°C) for 25 to 30 minutes until the skins crack and the nuts get a bit browned. Let them cool for about 20 minutes, then rub them in your hands or in a clean cloth to remove the skins. Place the still-warm skinned hazelnuts in the food processor and blend them on high speed to get hazelnut butter. It's important to use freshly roasted, still-warm hazelnuts—this is crucial.

You will probably need to stop blending once or twice, depending on how powerful your food processor is, to scrape the sides. Add all the remaining ingredients and continue blending until you get a smooth and shiny Nutella. Transfer it into a jar with a lid and enjoy with these yummy pancakes and anything else you wish.

You can store it in the refrigerator for up to 2 weeks.

To make the pancakes, mix the milk with the lemon juice in a small bowl. Set aside.

Sift the flour, baking powder, sugar, salt and vanilla, if using, into a medium-sized mixing bowl. Add the chia seeds and mix to combine.

Make a well in the center and add the oil and milk-lemon mixture. Mix gently until just combined. Coat the blueberries in 1 teaspoon of flour and add to the batter. Fold gently and let the batter sit for 5 to 10 minutes. Be careful not to overmix the batter; a few lumps of flour left is fine.

Heat ½ teaspoon of coconut oil in a large skillet on medium to low heat. Pour a scoop of the batter into the pan, letting it cook for 1½ to 2 minutes or until little bubbles start to form. It is important that not too much batter is left uncooked on top because it will spill while flipping and you will get flat pancakes. Flip the pancake and cook for 1 minute on the other side. Set it aside on the plate and continue until the batter is used up.

Serve pancakes with a dollop of Homemade Nutella and fresh berries.

BLUEBERRY BUCKLE

YIELD: 9 SLICES

A beautiful moist cake filled with juicy blueberries and topped with a yummy streusel topping, kind of a crossover between muffins and a coffee cake. This is a delicious addition to your breakfast or coffee ritual. Make this Blueberry Buckle a day in advance for the best flavor.

CAKE

1 tbsp (13 g) chia seeds

4 tbsp (60 ml) water

½ cup (120 ml) oat milk, room temperature

1 tsp apple cider vinegar

1½ cups (190 g) white spelt flour, plus 1 tbsp (10 g) to coat the blueberries (see Notes)

½ tsp baking powder

½ tsp baking soda

1 tsp vanilla powder or 2 tsp (10 ml) vanilla extract

¼ tsp fine Himalayan salt

1 tsp grated lemon zest

¼ cup (60 ml) melted coconut oil

¼ cup (60 ml) maple syrup (see Notes)

2 to 3 tbsp (30 to 45 ml) lemon juice

½ cup (75 g) blueberries, plus 1 tbsp (15 g) for topping

STREUSEL TOPPING

½ cup (50 g) old fashioned rolled oats

2 tbsp (25 g) almond meal

1 tbsp (15 ml) maple syrup

1 tbsp (15 ml) melted coconut oil

½ tsp lemon juice

Pinch of vanilla powder

Pinch of salt

Preheat the oven to 355°F (180°C) and prepare an 8 x 8–inch (20 x 20–cm) square pan by greasing the bottom and sides with coconut oil and lining the bottom, leaving the excess parchment paper on the sides to easily remove the cake. Grind the chia seeds using a coffee grinder or a small food processor and mix with the water in a small bowl. Leave it to thicken for 10 to 20 minutes.

Mix the milk with the apple cider vinegar and leave it to sour for 10 to 15 minutes. Sift the flour with the baking powder, baking soda, vanilla and salt into a large mixing bowl. Add the lemon zest.

In a separate bowl, whisk the oil, syrup and lemon juice. Add the oil mixture and chia egg to the flour mixture and fold gently with a silicone spatula or a large wooden spoon. Pour in the soured milk and keep folding gently until just combined. Do not overmix. It is fine if the batter looks a bit lumpy. Coat ½ cup (75 g) of blueberries with 1 tablespoon (10 g) of the flour and gently fold them into the batter. Transfer the batter into the prepared baking pan, smooth the surface with a spatula and scatter 1 tablespoon (15 g) of blueberries on top and press them gently into the batter.

To prepare the streusel topping, in a small bowl, mix the oats, almond meal, syrup, oil, lemon juice, vanilla and salt. Scatter the streusel over the top of the cake batter and press it gently into the batter.

Bake the cake in the preheated oven for 25 to 30 minutes. Check if it is done after 25 minutes; if the top is nicely browned and slightly cracked, pierce the center all the way through with a toothpick. If it comes out clean, with just a few moist crumbs attached, it is done. If there's any wet batter on it, keep baking for another 5 minutes and check again.

When it's done, take it out of the oven and put the pan on a cooling rack. Leave it to cool for 15 to 20 minutes. Then take the cake out of the pan and transfer it to the rack to cool down completely.

You can store the buckle in a sealed container or wrapped tightly in plastic wrap on a countertop for up to 3 days. To keep it longer, store the buckle in the refrigerator for up to 7 days or freeze for up to 1 month.

NOTES: Make this treat sweeter by adding a little bit more syrup to the cake recipe.

To make this Blueberry Buckle gluten free, substitute the spelt flour with half rice or buckwheat flour and half almond meal. You can also substitute the chia egg with a flax egg.

CRUNCHY BUCKWHEAT WAFFLES

GLUTEN FREE | YIELD: 6-8 WAFFLES

What sounds better than waking up to a stack of waffles, especially when you can smell the delicious fragrance of apples and cinnamon wafting from the kitchen? These beautifully crunchy waffles are a wonderful breakfast topped with nut butter and berries, or an indulgent dessert drizzled with some melted Homemade Dark Chocolate Coating (page 74). Or mix it up and add all three for a delicious and nutritious start to your day.

½ cup (50 g) old fashioned rolled oats (see Note)

1½ cups (235 g) buckwheat flour

1 tsp baking powder

½ tsp Himalayan salt

Pinch of vanilla powder, optional

½ tsp cinnamon

2 tbsp (25 g) chia seeds

1 cup (240 ml) almond or oat milk

⅔ cup (160 ml) water

2 tbsp (30 ml) maple syrup

3 tbsp (45 ml) melted coconut oil

1 tbsp (15 ml) lemon juice

1 cup (175 g) grated apple, about 2 small apples

FOR SERVING

Homemade Dark Chocolate Coating (page 74)

Nut butter or jam of choice

Fresh berries

Grind the oats in a coffee grinder or food processor. Place them in a mixing bowl and sift in the buckwheat flour, baking powder, salt, vanilla, if using, and cinnamon. Add the chia seeds.

In a small bowl, add the milk, water, syrup, oil and lemon juice. Using a whisk, fold the dry ingredients into the wet ingredients, resulting in a fairly smooth batter. Do not overmix. Fold in the grated apple.

Warm up the waffle maker and cook the waffles for 5 to 6 minutes. It is important not to open the waffle maker until at least 5 minutes into cooking, as the waffles will break apart and separate. Use 1 to 2 tablespoons (15 to 30 ml) of batter for each waffle, depending on the size of your waffle maker and how large or small you want them to be. Smaller waffles will be crunchier. If the waffles stick, brush the plates with some coconut oil. The waffles are done when they look slightly browned and crunchy without any uncooked batter visible.

Eat the waffles immediately with some Homemade Dark Chocolate Coating, peanut butter or jam and fresh berries.

NOTE: To ensure these are gluten free, be sure to use certified gluten-free oats in the recipe.

BERRY CRUMB BARS

GLUTEN FREE; NUT FREE | YIELD: 16 SLICES

These tender, crumbly bars with a juicy berry center and a crunchy topping are a super easy dessert that calls for almost no washing or chopping and no equipment but an oven. They are practically a nutritious sweet breakfast or a snack in the form of a delicious indulgent dessert. I love making them, especially in the summer when there's an abundance of berries and soft fruits of all kinds in season. Choose your own favorite fruit combination, or just one kind, and get to work. The only difficult part will be waiting for them to cool in the refrigerator for a few hours so they can be cut without making a mess.

CRUMBLE

1½ cups (150 g) old fashioned rolled oats (see Note)

1½ cups (220 g) buckwheat flour (see Note)

½ cup (65 g) coconut sugar

½ tsp baking powder

⅓ tsp Himalayan salt

½ cup (120 ml) melted extra virgin coconut oil

1 tsp vanilla extract or ½ tsp vanilla powder

2 tbsp (30 ml) maple syrup

1 tbsp (15 ml) lemon juice

FILLING

4 cups (600 g) mixed berries (see Notes)

⅓ cup plus 1 tbsp (55 g) coconut sugar

Pinch of salt

2 tbsp (30 ml) lemon juice

2 tbsp (20 g) tapioca starch

1 tbsp (15 g) buckwheat flour

Warm up the oven to 350°F (175°C). Line an 8-inch (20-cm) square pan with parchment paper, leaving some excess paper hanging on the sides to easily remove the bars.

Place the oats, flour, sugar, baking powder, salt, coconut oil, vanilla, syrup and lemon juice in a large mixing bowl. Using your hands, crumble the ingredients together. The mixture will seem a little dry but will hold when pressed together. To make the base, take two-thirds of the mixture and press down with your hands firmly on the bottom of the prepared pan. Using the flat bottom of a cup, press it even more firmly and level the sides. Bake it for 15 to 20 minutes until the edges are light golden brown.

To prepare the filling, place the berries into a large mixing bowl and add the sugar, salt, lemon juice, tapioca starch and flour and mix to coat the berries. Mash the berries with the back of a spoon while mixing. Spread the berry mixture evenly on the baked base and top with the reserved one-third of the crumble. Gently press it down.

Bake for another 30 to 35 minutes until the top is nice and golden and the fruits are bubbling. Remove it from the oven and allow the bars to cool down completely. I recommend that you refrigerate the bars for at least a few hours to firm them up before slicing. Store them in an airtight container for up to 7 days in the fridge.

NOTES: If using frozen berries, let them thaw and drain in a colander before seasoning them. Otherwise, the moisture released from them will make the bars soggy.

You can substitute the buckwheat flour with brown rice flour in the same amount; to substitute with all-purpose flour, use 1½ cups (190 g).

To ensure these are gluten free, be sure to use certified gluten-free oats in the recipe.

GOOEY CHOCOLATE CHIP MUG CAKE

GLUTEN FREE; NUT FREE | YIELD: 1 MUG CAKE

Incredibly moist and gooey, it is the best single-serving dessert to whip up in no time! This treat is perfect for times when you need a little something to satisfy your sweet tooth without the need to take out the mixing bowls and all the baking equipment. Just a spoon and a bowl will do it. Top this delicious little cake with some berry jam or Homemade Nutella (page 119) for an even more indulgent treat.

2 tbsp (30 ml) oat milk, room temperature

¼ tsp lemon juice

1 tbsp (15 ml) applesauce

1 tbsp (15 ml) maple syrup

1 tbsp (15 ml) melted extra virgin coconut oil

Pinch of vanilla powder, optional

3 tbsp (45 g) brown rice flour (see Note)

¼ tsp baking powder

Small pinch of salt

1 tbsp (20 g) vegan chocolate chips

TOPPINGS

Fruit jam

Homemade Nutella (page 119)

If using the oven, preheat to 350°F (175°C). Grease a small ramekin (for the oven) or mug (for the microwave) that is the size of about 1 cup (240 ml).

Mix together the milk and lemon juice in a small bowl. Leave it for 5 minutes to sour. Whisk in the applesauce, syrup and oil. Add the vanilla, if using, flour, baking powder and salt, and briefly fold until you get a relatively smooth batter. A few lumps of flour left is fine. Fold in the chocolate chips, reserving a few pieces for decoration.

Transfer the batter into the ramekin or mug, and scatter the reserved chocolate chips on top.

If using the oven, bake for 25 minutes, until the top is slightly cracked and browned around the edges. Check it after 22 to 23 minutes, and if it is done, the top will be slightly cracked. Insert a toothpick into the center, and if it comes out clean, the cake is done. If there's any batter on it, bake it for another few minutes and check again. When done, take it out on the cooling rack to cool for about 10 to 15 minutes, top with jam or Homemade Nutella and dig in!

If you want your cake to be done super quickly, you can microwave it for 1½ to 2 minutes.

NOTE: You can substitute brown rice flour with any of the following: buckwheat, white spelt flour, oat or unbleached all-purpose flour. To keep it gluten free, use buckwheat or certified gluten-free oat flour.

LEMONY STRAWBERRY STREUSEL MUFFINS

GLUTEN FREE | YIELD: 12 MUFFINS

These soft muffins are gluten free and a wonderful indulgent breakfast or a snack, but also a light everyday dessert. The addition of strawberries makes them super moist and fragrant, while the streusel topping adds some crunchiness to the experience.

½ cup (120 ml) oat milk, room temperature

1 tsp apple cider vinegar

1 tbsp (15 g) golden flax seeds

3 tbsp (45 ml) water

1 cup (140 g) brown rice flour, plus more to coat strawberries

2 tbsp (20 g) tapioca starch

½ tsp baking soda

½ tsp baking powder

⅓ tsp Himalayan salt

½ to 1 tsp vanilla powder or 1 to 2 tsp (5 to 10 ml) vanilla extract

1 tsp grated lemon zest

⅓ cup (80 ml) maple or agave syrup (see Notes)

¼ cup (60 ml) extra virgin olive oil

2 tbsp (30 ml) lemon juice

1 cup (135 g) strawberries, halved or quartered depending on the size

STREUSEL TOPPING

½ cup (50 g) old fashioned rolled oats (see Notes)

1 tbsp (15 ml) extra virgin olive oil

2 tbsp (30 ml) maple syrup

2 tsp (10 ml) lemon juice

Pinch of salt

Pinch of vanilla powder

Preheat the oven to 355°F (180°C). Line a 12-cup muffin pan with silicone or paper liners. If using paper liners, grease them with some oil to prevent sticking. It works best if you use coconut or olive oil spray.

Mix the milk with the vinegar and leave it to sour for 10 to 15 minutes. To make the flax egg, grind the flax seeds using a coffee grinder or a small food processor and mix with the water in a small bowl. Set it aside to thicken.

In a separate bowl, mix together the ingredients for the streusel topping and set it aside.

Sift the flour, tapioca starch, baking soda, baking powder, salt and vanilla into a large mixing bowl. Mix in the lemon zest.

In a small bowl, add the syrup, oil and lemon juice. Whisk them to incorporate and add them to the flour mixture, along with the flax egg. Fold gently with a silicone spatula or a large wooden spoon. Pour in the soured milk and keep folding gently until just combined. The batter should be a bit lumpy with few flour pockets left. Don't overmix. In a separate bowl, coat two-thirds of the strawberries with some flour and gently fold them into the batter.

Evenly divide the batter into the muffin cups. Each muffin cup will be two-thirds full. Top each muffin with reserved strawberries and the streusel topping.

Bake the muffins in the oven for about 15 minutes, until they have risen nicely, and the streusel topping is nicely browned on the edges. Check if the muffins are done by inserting a toothpick in the middle. It should come out clean, with just a few moist crumbs attached.

When done, remove them from the oven and allow them to cool slightly in the pan, for about 5 minutes, then transfer the muffins onto a wire rack. Let them cool for about 20 minutes and enjoy warm.

You can store them in a closed container at room temperature for up to 3 days.

NOTES: These are a little on the sweet side, so if you'd like things less sweet, you can reduce the syrup to ¼ cup (60 ml).

To ensure these are gluten free, be sure to use certified gluten-free oats in the recipe.

BUCKWHEAT HAZELNUT *and* CHOCOLATE BLISS BALLS

GLUTEN FREE | YIELD: 30 BLISS BALLS

These little gems will steal your heart. They are so chocolaty and rich, you'd never believe there was anything healthy in them. But they are also incredibly rich in healthy protein, fats, carbohydrates and fiber. They're great as a pre- or post-workout snack that will give you energy and nourishment, without weighing you down. Keep them in the refrigerator for when you feel a little peckish or are just a bit hungry and not in the mood for making anything. They keep great at room temperature thanks to buckwheat and cocoa butter, which is much more stable compared to coconut oil. This also means you can take them with you wherever you go!

⅓ cup (60 g) raw buckwheat

2 pinches of fine Himalayan salt, divided

¼ cup (35 g) unrefined cocoa butter

½ heaping cup plus 2 tbsp (100 g) roasted hazelnuts

½ cup (130 g) tightly packed pitted, chopped dates

½ tsp vanilla or 1 tsp vanilla extract

½ cup (50 g) unsweetened cocoa powder

1 tsp lemon juice

1 tbsp (15 ml) maple syrup, optional for sweeter truffles

⅓ cup (45 g) whole roasted hazelnuts (roughly 1 for each truffle, about 30 nuts)

Wash, drain and place the buckwheat in a small pan. Add three times as much water and bring to a boil. Add a pinch of salt and cook, covered and on the lowest flame, for 15 to 20 minutes, or until soft. Set it aside to cool.

Melt the cocoa butter in a double boiler and set it aside to cool.

Grind the hazelnuts in a food processor, remove 2 tablespoons (10 g) to a small bowl for rolling the bliss balls, and set aside.

Measure ⅔ cup (150 g) of cooled, cooked buckwheat and add it to the ground hazelnuts in the food processor. Continue processing briefly. Add the dates and continue processing. The mixture should be starting to resemble a sticky dough. Add the melted cocoa butter, a pinch of salt, vanilla, cocoa powder and lemon juice and continue processing briefly. You should have a sticky and smooth dough. Taste the dough and add 1 tablespoon (15 ml) of maple syrup for more sweetness if needed.

Refrigerate the dough for 15 to 20 minutes to firm up a bit, as it will be easier to roll it into neat balls.

Take pieces of dough and roll into walnut-sized balls. Press a whole hazelnut into each, then roll them in ground hazelnuts.

Keep the bliss balls refrigerated in a closed container for up to 10 days.

NOTE: Feel free to customize these! Make them bigger or smaller, with or without hazelnuts in the center (though I highly recommend them) or roll them in cocoa powder or shredded coconut.

WALNUT *and* CARAMEL CHOCOLATE BARS

GLUTEN FREE; GRAIN FREE | YIELD: 12–14 BARS

These powerful slices are super indulgent and one of my favorite wholesome healthy snacks that feel super naughty and decadent. They taste just like chocolate bars, or even better. Make them and wrap them in individual portions and keep them on hand for a quick nutritious pick-me-up or a sugar-cravings fix.

BASE LAYER

1½ cups (220 g) cashews

1 cup (140 g) almonds

Pinch of Himalayan salt

3 tbsp (45 ml) melted extra virgin coconut oil

3 tbsp (45 ml) maple syrup

CARAMEL WALNUT LAYER

2 cups (310 g) pitted dates, softened (see Note)

3 tbsp (45 ml) melted extra virgin coconut oil

Pinch of salt

1 tsp vanilla extract

⅔ cup (70 g) walnut halves

Homemade Dark Chocolate Coating (page 74)

Line an 8-inch (20-cm) square pan with parchment paper, leaving some paper hanging over the sides.

To make the base layer, place cashews and almonds in a food processor and grind finely. Add the salt, oil and syrup and pulse until you get a wet, sticky and crumbly dough. Press the dough firmly into the prepared pan. Place in the freezer or refrigerator to chill while you prepare the date caramel.

To make the caramel, place the dates in the food processor, add the oil, salt and vanilla and blend to get a thick smooth paste. Smooth the caramel over the chilled base and arrange the walnut halves neatly on top. Place it again in the refrigerator.

Make one batch of the homemade chocolate according to the instructions on page 74. Pour the chocolate over the walnuts and caramel and shake the pan to smooth the chocolate.

Return the pan to the refrigerator to firm up for at least 2 to 3 hours.

Keep the bars refrigerated or freeze in a sealed container, as they will be too soft at room temperature. They will keep in the refrigerator for up to 2 weeks, and in the freezer for up to 4 months. You can also cut them into bars and keep them wrapped in foil. This is the best way to freeze them; just let the bars thaw at room temperature for 15 to 20 minutes before digging in!

NOTE: When we're making date caramel, the dates should be soaked in hot water for at least 15 minutes to soften. Drain them and gently squeeze out the excess liquid before use.

SUPER INDULGENT
NO-BAKE AND RAW TREATS

No-bake and raw treats are so incredibly rich in flavor and consistency, some would even say they are sinfully decadent.

In my experience, they are so good that they appeal enormously to everyone, even to non-vegans, who cannot even tell the difference between these and conventional dairy-, sugar- and egg-loaded desserts. They usually say that these are pure heaven, and they cannot believe that they're also vegan and wholesome!

Another great thing about no-bake and raw treats is that they're fairly easy and quick to make, usually in under 30 minutes. You just need a blender and/or a food processor, and the method is just to throw everything in, blend, place in a pan and freeze. The only tough part is waiting for them to set so you can dig in. Stopping yourself from finishing them in one sitting could be another issue. But I'm sure you can do it.

I recommend making my raw cakes at least a day in advance, especially the cakes that call for coconut oil. Even though the cake will firm up and set in 6 to 12 hours, it will still keep firming up in the following days to get that perfectly firm cake and sharp sliced edges. All these raw treats also freeze perfectly, so they can be made even further in advance and stuck out of the way in your freezer for unexpected guests or your own future cravings.

A FEW NOTES TO KEEP IN MIND:

- In these treats, I use melted coconut oil as well as melted cocoa butter. Be sure that the other ingredients you're adding are not cold, or else the coconut oil or cocoa butter will solidify and make the blending process more difficult.

- The biggest difference between coconut oil and cocoa butter, besides the obvious difference in flavor, is their performance in setting fillings. Cocoa butter is much more stable at room temperature and it will make any filling set better. I've specified in the ingredients lists where it's important to use cocoa butter.

- Always use the smaller amount of water suggested in the ingredient lists first, as the cakes will set better with this amount, and then only add the rest if needed to blend the fillings into a creamy and smooth consistency.

- Most of the cake bases and fillings are interchangeable. For instance, if you prefer a grain-free base and you'd like to make White Chocolate Raspberry Swirl No-Bake Cake (page 147), you can swap the base from the Raw Strawberry and Lemon Cake (page 150), which is grain free. Or you can adapt the base ingredients to your preferences or to what you have at hand. Feel free to swap nuts (e.g., almonds for walnuts or cashews) and seeds (e.g., sunflower seeds for pumpkin seeds) as desired to make your own versions.

- Many of the following recipes call for soft dates. Several types of dates come in a softened state, but if you have tougher dates, feel free to soak them first. Just make sure to drain the dates and release any excess water before starting the recipes (see Note on page 132).

NUTELLA CAKE

My favorite classic and one of the first raw cakes I ever made—I've served this at too many parties to count. My favorite comment was: "I think I just died and went to chocolate heaven!" It features such incredibly rich chocolate and hazelnut flavor with the marvelous crunchiness of the base contrasting with the smooth creamy filling. Pure heaven!

½ cup plus 1 tbsp (80 g) unrefined cocoa butter, divided

BASE

1½ cups (215 g) roasted hazelnuts

2 pinches of Himalayan salt

4 tbsp (60 ml) maple syrup

1 tsp lemon juice

3 tbsp (30 g) unsweetened cocoa powder

FILLING

1 heaping cup (150 g) softened cashews (see Note on page 16)

½ cup (80 g) roasted hazelnuts

½ cup (120 ml) water

4 to 5 tbsp (60 to 75 ml) maple syrup

2 tsp (10 ml) lemon juice

½ tsp vanilla powder or 1 tsp vanilla extract

Pinch of Himalayan salt

½ cup (50 g) unsweetened cocoa powder

Melt the cocoa butter in a double boiler and set it aside to cool.

Prepare an 8-inch (20-cm) round springform pan by lining the bottom with parchment paper.

To make the base, grind the hazelnuts in a food processor and add the salt, syrup, lemon juice and 2 tablespoons (30 ml) of melted cocoa butter. Continue processing.

Next, add the cocoa powder and pulse until a sticky dough is formed. I like keeping it a bit crunchy, with small bits of hazelnuts left for that delicious bite. Remove the dough from the food processor, and press it firmly into the prepared pan and smooth it out. Place it in the freezer to chill while you prepare the filling.

Wash and drain the cashews, place them in a high-speed blender and add the hazelnuts, water, syrup, lemon juice, vanilla and salt. Blend until smooth. Add the remaining melted cocoa butter and cocoa powder and continue blending until the filling is completely smooth and creamy. If it is too thick to blend, add a little bit of water. Be careful not to add too much, as the filling might become too runny and will not firm up. Feel free to add more vanilla, cocoa powder or syrup to taste.

Pour the filling on the chilled base, shake the pan gently and tap it on the countertop to smooth the top and release any trapped air bubbles. You can decorate it with some chopped or ground hazelnuts, if desired.

Cover and refrigerate the cake for at least 6 hours. I recommend chilling overnight, if possible. If you're in a hurry, you can speed things up by placing it into a freezer for 3 to 4 hours to set faster.

It will keep in the refrigerator in a sealed container for up to 10 days. You can also freeze it for up to 4 months. Thaw the cake in the refrigerator for at least 1 hour or 30 minutes at room temperature.

RAW BLUEBERRY CAKE

GLUTEN FREE; GRAIN FREE | YIELD: 1 (9.5-INCH [24-CM]) ROUND CAKE; 12-14 SLICES

While the color of this cake is breathtaking, so is the flavor—delicious blueberries, fragrant vanilla and a hint of coconut come together just perfectly. It is amazing how little work invested makes such a fantastic result. Whenever I made it for birthdays and parties, it was a huge success, especially among the fruit-cake lovers. Blitz it up for your guests and you will be considered a cake goddess!

BASE

1 cup (135 g) sunflower seeds (see Notes)

1½ cups (215 g) almonds

3 tbsp (45 ml) melted extra virgin coconut oil (see Notes)

2 pinches of salt

1 tsp lemon juice

Pinch of vanilla powder or ½ tsp vanilla extract

⅔ cup (120 g) soft pitted dates

FILLING

2 heaping cups (300 g) soaked cashews (see Note on page 16)

2 cups (300 g) blueberries

½ cup (120 ml) agave or maple syrup

3 tbsp (45 ml) lemon juice

½ tsp vanilla powder or 1 tsp vanilla extract

Pinch of salt

½ cup (120 ml) melted extra virgin coconut oil

Line the bottom of a 9.5-inch (24-cm) round springform pan with parchment paper.

Grind the sunflower seeds and almonds in a food processor and add the oil, salt, lemon juice and vanilla and continue processing. Add the dates and process until a sticky dough is formed. I like keeping the base a bit crunchy, with small bits of nuts left. Remove the dough from the food processor, and press it into the prepared pan, smooth it out and place it in the freezer to chill while you prepare the filling.

Wash and drain the cashews and place them in a high-speed blender. Add the blueberries, syrup, lemon juice, vanilla, salt and oil. Blend until the filling is completely smooth and creamy. If it is too thick to blend, add a little bit of water (1 tablespoon [15 ml]) or a handful more of blueberries. In this base, blended blueberries stand in instead of liquid (water). Be careful not to add too much, as the filling might become too runny and will not firm up properly.

Pour the prepared filling on the chilled base, shake the pan gently and tap it on the countertop to smooth the top and eliminate any air bubbles.

Cover and refrigerate the cake for at least 6 hours. I recommend chilling it overnight, if possible. It doesn't need to be put in a freezer, but if you're in a hurry, you can place it there to shorten the setting time to 4 hours. Serve the cake directly from the refrigerator. The cake will become firmer the longer it is left in the refrigerator.

It will keep refrigerated in a sealed container for up to 10 days. You can also freeze it for up to 4 months. Thaw the cake in the refrigerator for at least an hour or 20 to 30 minutes at room temperature.

NOTES: You can toast the sunflower seeds for an even more delicious cake base. Toast them on low to medium heat until they are fragrant. Let them cool down completely before processing.

Feel free to substitute the sunflower seeds with walnuts, cashews or pecans or increase the amount of almonds accordingly.

I prefer using extra virgin coconut oil, but if you mind the taste of coconut, feel free to use odorless coconut oil.

DOUBLE CHOCOLATE CAKE

GLUTEN FREE; GRAIN FREE | YIELD: 1 (8-INCH [20-CM]) CAKE; 10-12 SLICES

This cake is so decadently rich—a beautiful creamy dark chocolate filling with just a hint of vanilla and coffee resting on a crunchy chocolate almond base. The simplicity of raw cakes is one of the cool things about them; they're perfect when you need a fancy dessert and have no time or energy, as it's amazing how fast this baby is done—it literally takes me 20 minutes. Then all that is left to do is to wait for it to set.

½ cup (70 g) cocoa paste (see Notes), divided

CRUST

2 cups (290 g) whole almonds

1 cup (190 g) pitted dates

2 tbsp (30 ml) melted extra virgin coconut oil

⅓ tsp vanilla powder or ½ tsp vanilla extract

Pinch of salt

2 tbsp (20 g) unsweetened cocoa powder

FILLING

2 cups (280 g) soaked cashews (see Note on page 16)

½ to ⅔ cup (120 to 160 ml) water

½ cup (120 ml) agave syrup

1 tsp freshly squeezed lemon juice

½ tsp vanilla powder or 1 tsp vanilla extract

Pinch of salt

1 tsp instant coffee powder, optional

OPTIONAL TOPPINGS

Fresh berries

Sliced almonds

Chocolate chunks

Line the bottom of an 8-inch (20-cm) round springform pan with parchment paper. Melt the cocoa paste in a double boiler. Set it aside to cool.

To make the crust, roughly grind the almonds in a food processor. Chop the dates and add them to the almonds. Add the coconut oil and keep pulsing until you get a sticky dough. Add the vanilla, salt, cocoa powder and 2 tablespoons (30 ml) of melted cocoa paste and keep pulsing until a sticky dough is formed. Transfer it into the prepared pan and push it firmly to form the base, leaving the edges slightly raised. Use a tablespoon to press and level the base, then push even more firmly and shape the elevated edges using the flat bottom of a cup. Place it in the refrigerator while you prepare the filling.

To make the filling, wash and drain the cashews. Put them in the blender, starting with ½ cup (120 ml) of water and add the syrup, lemon juice, vanilla, salt and instant coffee powder, if using; blend until smooth. Add the reserved cocoa paste and continue blending. If it's too thick, gradually add the reserved water and keep blending until you get a smooth, creamy filling. Check it for sweetness and if it's chocolaty enough. You can add more syrup and additional unsweetened cocoa powder to taste. Pour the filling on top of the crust. Shake it gently and pat on the countertop to even the top and release any air bubbles. Cover and place the cake in the freezer for 2 hours and then transfer it to the refrigerator for another 4 to 6 hours. It will become firmer the longer it is left in the refrigerator. You can decorate it with berries or almonds and chocolate, if using.

Store it in a sealed container in the refrigerator for up to 1 week. You can also store it in the freezer for up to 3 months. To serve it, defrost for about 30 minutes at room temperature.

NOTES: If you can't get cocoa paste, you can use unrefined cocoa butter instead. In that case, you need to add an extra 1 tablespoon (10 g) of unsweetened cocoa powder to the base and ½ cup (50 g) to the filling.

WHITE AND DARK CHOCOLATE CAKE
with RASPBERRY CHIA JAM

GLUTEN FREE; GRAIN FREE | YIELD: 1 (8-INCH [20-CM]) ROUND CAKE; 10-12 SLICES

This combination of creamy double chocolate filling, rich chocolate base and tangy raspberry jam is just irresistible. The crunchiness of the intensely chocolate base beautifully complements the softness and lightness of the chocolate filling layers, while the raspberry jam adds that gorgeous zing and cuts through the richness of all the chocolate. I highly recommend you trying this raspberry-chocolate combo, because you might just fall in love with it.

½ cup plus 2 tbsp (90 g) unrefined cocoa butter (see Note)

RASPBERRY CHIA JAM
2 cups (280 g) raspberries

2 tbsp (30 ml) agave or maple syrup

Pinch of salt

1½ tbsp (20 g) chia seeds

BASE
2 cups (290 g) almonds

2 pinches of salt

1 cup (175 g) dates, pitted and softened

2 tbsp (20 g) unsweetened cocoa powder

FILLING
2 heaping cups (300 g) soaked cashews (see Note on page 16)

½ cup (120 ml) agave syrup

Pinch of fine salt

½ tsp vanilla powder or 1 tsp vanilla extract

½ to ⅔ cup (120 to 160 ml) water

5 tbsp (50 g) unsweetened cocoa powder

Line the bottom of an 8-inch (20-cm) round springform pan with parchment paper. Melt the cocoa butter in a double boiler and set it aside to cool.

To prepare the raspberry jam, place the raspberries in a small pan and add the syrup and salt. Cook them covered over a low flame for about 10 minutes, occasionally stirring and crushing the berries until they are soft and falling apart. Add the chia seeds and stir a few times more until the sauce starts thickening. Remove it from the stove, cover and leave it to thicken and cool down.

To make the base, place the almonds in a food processor and roughly grind them. Add the salt, dates, cocoa powder and 2 tablespoons (30 ml) of melted cocoa butter. Keep pulsing until you get a sticky dough. It shouldn't be completely smooth and instead have some nutty bits left inside.

Press the dough firmly into the bottom of the prepared pan to form a base, with the edges slightly elevated so the jam will stay safely confined inside the cake. Use a tablespoon to press and level the base, then push even more firmly and shape the elevated edges using the flat bottom of a cup. Spoon in the prepared jam and place into the freezer to chill until the filling is ready.

To prepare the layers of filling, place the soaked, washed and drained cashews in the blender, add the syrup, salt, vanilla, remaining melted cocoa butter and ½ cup (120 ml) of water, reserving the rest, and blend until smooth. If it is too thick to blend keep adding a little bit of reserved water. It is better to add as little as possible to make the filling set better and to get nice clean slices of cake.

(continued)

NOTE: Cocoa butter should be organic and unrefined, so it has a gorgeous chocolate smell and aroma. Refined cocoa butter will not!

Pour half of the filling over the jam and base, shake the pan to smooth the top and pat gently on the countertop a few times to release any air bubbles. Place it back in the freezer to set partially so you can pour the second layer of filling on top; this will take around 30 minutes.

For the remaining filling, add the cocoa powder and fold in with a spatula or blend until smooth. Pour it very carefully over the chilled white chocolate layer, starting around the edges, as it will still not be very firm. Gently shake the pan to smooth out the top. Cover and refrigerate to set for at least 8 hours or overnight. If you're in a hurry, you can chill it in the freezer for 5 to 6 hours.

The cake will become firmer the longer it is left in the refrigerator. If you make it in advance and leave to set and cool for at least a day or two, you will get perfectly sharp slices of this delicious cake. It will keep in the refrigerator in a sealed container for up to 10 days. You can also freeze it for up to 4 months. Thaw it in the refrigerator for at least 1 hour or 30 minutes at room temperature.

WHITE CHOCOLATE RASPBERRY SWIRL NO-BAKE CAKE

GLUTEN FREE | YIELD: 1 (8-INCH [20-CM]) CAKE; 10-12 SLICES

Who else loves the combination of raspberries and chocolate? I'm especially a fan of white chocolate and raspberries, and in this no-bake cake, it comes together with the beautiful creaminess of the filling, tanginess of the raspberry sauce swirl and the crunchiness of the nut base.

RASPBERRY SWIRL

2 cups (200 g) frozen raspberries

2 tbsp (30 ml) agave or maple syrup

Pinch of Himalayan salt

½ tsp tapioca starch

1 tbsp (15 ml) water

BASE

½ cup plus 2 tbsp (90 g) unrefined cocoa butter, divided (see Notes)

1½ cups (215 g) almonds (see Notes)

½ cup (50 g) oats (see Notes)

2 pinches of salt

1 cup (175 g) pitted dates, softened

1 tsp lemon juice

½ tsp vanilla

FILLING

2 cups (280 g) cashews (see Note on page 16)

2 tbsp (30 ml) lemon juice

½ cup (120 ml) agave syrup

Pinch of salt

½ tsp vanilla powder or 1 tsp vanilla extract

½ to ⅔ cup (120 to 160 ml) water

Line the bottom of an 8-inch (20-cm) round springform pan with parchment paper.

To prepare the raspberries, place them in a small saucepan and add the syrup and salt. Cook them covered over a low flame until melted and soft, around 10 minutes. Dilute the tapioca starch with the water and add the mixture into the raspberries, stirring constantly and crushing the berries with the spoon. Remove the berries from the flame and set them aside to cool down completely.

Melt the cocoa butter in a double boiler and set it aside to cool down.

In a food processor, roughly grind the almonds then add the oats, salt, dates, lemon juice, 2 tablespoons (30 ml) of the melted cocoa butter and vanilla. Keep pulsing until you get a sticky, crumbly dough that holds together when pressed between your fingers. Transfer it into the prepared pan and press firmly into the base. Use a tablespoon to press and level the base, then push even more firmly and shape the elevated edges using the flat bottom of a cup. Chill it in the freezer until the filling is ready.

To make the filling, place the cashews in the blender, add the lemon juice, syrup, salt, vanilla, remaining melted cocoa butter and ½ cup (120 ml) of water. Blend the ingredients. If the mixture is too thick and won't blend, keep adding the reserved water. It is important not to add too much liquid, because then the filling will not firm up properly.

When the filling is creamy and smooth, pour half over the chilled base. Mix 3 to 4 tablespoons (45 to 60 ml) of raspberries into the other half and pour it on top. Take another 1 or 2 tablespoons (15 to 30 ml) of sauce and swirl it on the top, as desired.

(continued)

NOTES: Same as in other raw cakes, you can substitute almonds with some other nuts like cashews, walnuts, pecans and pistachios. To make it grain free, take out the oats from the base and use an equal amount of nuts, almonds or some other kind of nut.

Cocoa butter should be organic and unrefined, so it has a gorgeous chocolate smell and aroma. Refined cocoa butter will not!

Shake the pan to smooth the top and tap it on the countertop to release air bubbles from the filling. Cover and place the cake in the refrigerator for at least 6 hours or overnight to set and firm up.

If in a hurry, you can chill it in the freezer for 3 to 4 hours. The cake will become firmer the longer it is left in the refrigerator. If you make it in advance and leave it to set and cool for at least a day or two, you will get perfectly sharp slices of this delicious cake.

Use a sharp knife to cut it into slices and serve with more raspberry sauce. It will keep in the refrigerator in a sealed container for up to 10 days. You can also freeze it for up to 4 months. Thaw it in the refrigerator for at least 1 hour or 30 minutes at room temperature before serving.

RAW STRAWBERRY *and* LEMON CAKE

GLUTEN FREE; GRAIN FREE | YIELD: 1 (8-INCH [20-CM]) ROUND CAKE; 10–12 SLICES

This strawberry cake is a flavor explosion—you bite into soft strawberry filling rounded with lemon zest, coconut, vanilla and cinnamon before hitting a delicious rich and crunchy base that is simply divine. This winning cake will impress everyone!

BASE

1 cup (140 g) almonds

½ cup (50 g) walnuts

½ cup (75 g) pitted and chopped dates

3 tbsp (45 ml) melted extra virgin coconut oil (see Notes)

2 tsp (10 ml) lemon juice

Pinch of salt

Pinch of vanilla powder

Zest of 1 organic lemon

FILLING

2 cups (280 g) soaked cashews (see Note on page 16)

3 cups (390 g) fresh strawberries

4 tbsp (60 ml) lemon juice (see Notes)

½ cup (120 ml) agave or maple syrup

1 tsp vanilla powder or 1 tbsp (15 ml) vanilla extract

¼ tsp cinnamon

Pinch of ground ginger

Pinch of salt

½ cup (120 ml) melted extra virgin coconut oil

½ tsp lemon zest, optional

Prepare an 8-inch (20-cm) round springform pan by lining the bottom with parchment paper. Grind the almonds and walnuts in a food processor, then add the dates, oil, lemon juice, salt, vanilla and lemon zest and continue processing until a sticky dough is formed. I like keeping the base a bit crunchy, with small bits of nuts left inside to add an extra delicious bite to it.

Use a tablespoon to press and level the base, then push even more firmly and shape the elevated edges using the flat bottom of a cup. Place the prepared base in the freezer to chill while you prepare the filling.

To make the filling, place cashews in a high-speed blender. Add the strawberries, lemon juice, syrup, vanilla, cinnamon, ginger, salt and oil and blend until the filling is completely smooth and creamy. If it is too thick to blend, add a little bit of water, 1 tablespoon (15 ml) at the time, or more strawberries. Be careful not to add too much, as the filling might become too runny and will not firm up.

Feel free to add more vanilla or syrup to taste. You can add some lemon zest to the filling as well for even more intense citrusy flavor. Pour the filling onto the chilled base, shake the pan gently and tap it on the countertop to smooth the top and eliminate any air bubbles.

Cover and refrigerate the cake for at least 6 hours. I recommend chilling it overnight, if possible. If you're in a hurry, you can shorten the setting time to 4 hours by chilling in the freezer.

Slice it using a sharp knife and serve straight from the refrigerator.

Keep the cake in the refrigerator in a sealed container for up to 10 days. You can also freeze it for up to 4 months. Thaw it in the refrigerator for at least 1 hour or 30 minutes at room temperature before slicing and serving.

NOTES: I prefer using extra virgin coconut oil, but if you mind the taste of coconut, feel free to use odorless coconut oil.

Don't forget to zest the lemon before you juice it.

WALNUT *and* FIG SLICES

GLUTEN FREE; GRAIN FREE | YIELD: 9–16 SLICES

Figs are my summer love. Okay, I admit . . . I have quite a few summer loves but my connection to figs is special. I love them whether they're fresh or dried, as a small snack, or with chia pudding for breakfast or in desserts like these fabulous indulgent slices. They are such a perfect combination of tangy vanilla frosting, luscious fresh figs and an intensely sweet and rich dry fig and walnut base. Who could resist biting into them? Not me!

BASE

1 cup (140 g) cashews

1 cup (100 g) walnuts

1 cup (190 g) dried figs

½ cup (40 g) shredded coconut

1 tbsp (15 ml) melted extra virgin coconut oil (see Note on page 150)

3 pinches of fine Himalayan salt

1 tsp vanilla powder or 2 tsp (10 ml) vanilla extract

1 tsp lemon zest

2 tbsp (30 ml) lemon juice

FILLING

½ cup (75 g) cashews (see Note on page 16)

¼ cup (60 ml) agave syrup

1 tbsp (6 g) lemon zest

2 tbsp (30 ml) lemon juice

¼ cup (60 ml) melted extra virgin coconut oil

1 tsp vanilla powder or 2 tsp (10 ml) extract

Pinch of Himalayan salt

¼ tsp cinnamon

¼ cup (60 ml) water

1 cup (300 g) whole fresh figs to decorate, about 8 small figs

NOTE: I prefer using extra virgin coconut oil but if you mind the taste of coconut, feel free to use odorless coconut oil.

Preheat the oven to 300°F (150°C). Place the nuts on a baking sheet and roast for about 15 minutes or until fragrant and lightly browned on the edges. Keep an eye on them after 10 minutes of roasting, as they can easily burn. Set them aside to cool down completely.

Line an 8-inch (20-cm) baking dish with parchment paper, leaving the surplus to hang over the edges.

To make the base, chop the dried figs into small pieces to ease the blending as they can be pretty tough. Grind the cooled roasted nuts in a food processor and add the chopped figs, coconut, oil, salt, vanilla, lemon zest and lemon juice. Continue processing until you get a sticky soft dough that holds together when pressed between your fingers.

Press it evenly and firmly on the bottom of the dish to make the base. Place in the freezer or refrigerator while you make the filling.

To make the filling, wash and drain the soaked cashews, place them in the blender with the syrup, lemon zest, lemon juice, oil, vanilla, salt, cinnamon and water. Blend until creamy and smooth. If the mixture is too thick to blend, stir the mixture and add a little bit of water, 1 tablespoon (15 ml) at the time, and continue blending. Be careful not to add too much water, as the filling might be too runny and will not set in the refrigerator.

When ready, pour the filling over the chilled base, shake the dish gently and tap it on the countertop to smooth the top and eliminate any air bubbles. Cover it and refrigerate for 1 hour.

To decorate the cake, slice the fresh figs into thin slices and arrange them to cover the filling. Return it to the refrigerator to set for at least 6 hours. I recommend leaving it to set overnight if possible. If you're in a hurry, you can speed things up by placing it in the freezer for 3 to 4 hours.

Serve straight from the refrigerator, as the slices will soften if left at room temperature.

These will keep in the refrigerator in a sealed container for up to 10 days. You can also freeze them for up to 4 months. Thaw in the refrigerator for at least 30 to 45 minutes or 20 minutes at room temperature before serving.

PECAN SALTED CARAMEL SLICES

GLUTEN FREE | YIELD: 12–14 BARS

These delicious no-bake slices are such a guilt-free treat, loaded with plant goodness, healthy fats and protein, while also being gluten free. Have them as a healthy treat or a delicious post-workout power snack or a sweet addition to any meal, at home or on the go.

BASE

1½ cups (220 g) cashews

1 cup (145 g) peeled unsalted pistachios

4 tbsp (35 g) old fashioned rolled oats (see Notes)

Pinch of Himalayan salt

3 tbsp (45 ml) melted extra virgin coconut oil (see Notes)

2 tbsp (30 ml) maple syrup

SALTED CARAMEL

2 cups (310 g) tightly packed pitted dates, softened and drained (see Notes)

3 tbsp (45 ml) melted extra virgin coconut oil

1 tsp light miso paste or 2 pinches of salt

1 tsp vanilla powder

1 cup (100 g) pecan nuts

CHOCOLATE

2 tbsp (25 g) unrefined cocoa butter (see Notes)

2 tbsp (30 ml) maple syrup

⅓ cup (30 g) unsweetened cocoa powder

3 tbsp (45 ml) oat or almond milk, at room temperature

Line an 8-inch (20-cm) square pan with parchment paper, leaving the surplus hanging over the sides.

Place the cashews, pistachios and oats in a food processor and grind finely. Add the salt, oil and syrup and pulse until you get a wet, sticky and crumbly dough. Press the dough firmly into a prepared pan. Use a tablespoon to press and level the base, then push even more firmly and shape the edges using the flat bottom of a cup. Place it in the freezer or refrigerator to firm up while you make the salted caramel.

To make the salted caramel, drain the dates and gently squeeze out any extra water. Then place the dates in the food processor and add the oil, miso paste and vanilla. Process it to get a thick smooth paste.

Smooth the caramel over the chilled base and arrange the pecans neatly on top. Push them in gently. Refrigerate again.

To make the chocolate, melt the cocoa butter in a double boiler, remove it from the flame and add the syrup and cocoa powder, whisking until smooth. Add the milk gradually while still whisking constantly until you get a smooth consistency again. Pour the chocolate into a small pitcher and pour it over the pecans and caramel, forming a chocolate grid.

Return the pan to the refrigerator to firm up for at least 2 to 3 hours. Cut it with a sharp knife into slices or bars and serve directly from the refrigerator.

You can keep it unsliced in a sealed container in the refrigerator for up to 10 days. You can also cut it into bars and keep them individually wrapped in plastic foil. Freeze the bars for up to 4 months. To serve, allow them to thaw at room temperature for 10 to 15 minutes.

NOTES: To ensure these are gluten free, be sure to use certified gluten-free oats in the recipe.

I prefer using extra virgin coconut oil, but if you mind the taste of coconut, feel free to use odorless coconut oil. Cocoa butter should be organic and unrefined, so it has a gorgeous chocolate smell and aroma. Refined cocoa butter will not!

Soak the dates in warm water for at least half an hour to soften before starting the recipe.

INDIVIDUAL NEAPOLITAN CHEESECAKES

GLUTEN FREE | YIELD: 6 SMALL (8 OZ [250 ML]) JARS

Cheesecake made easy! I wanted to create a Neapolitan flavor combination, so I went for this trio of smooth vanilla cheesecake, crunchy homemade chocolate and tangy and fragrant strawberry coulis. You can use any cup or jar on hand and even take them with you to work or a picnic.

BASE

½ cup (70 g) almonds

¼ cup (25 g) old fashioned rolled oats (see Notes)

2 pinches of salt

1 tbsp (15 ml) melted extra virgin coconut oil

1 tbsp (15 ml) maple syrup

CHOCOLATE

2 tbsp (20 g) coconut oil

1 tbsp (15 ml) maple syrup

3 tbsp (30 g) unsweetened cocoa powder

3 tbsp (45 ml) plant milk

Pinch of salt

Pinch of vanilla powder

VANILLA CHEESECAKE

1 cup (140 g) soaked cashews (see Note on page 16)

2 tbsp (30 ml) lemon juice

¼ cup (60 ml) agave or maple syrup

½ tsp vanilla powder or 1 tsp vanilla extract

Pinch of salt

¼ to ⅓ cup (60 to 80 ml) water

¼ cup (60 ml) melted extra virgin coconut oil

STRAWBERRY COULIS

½ cup (70 g) whole strawberries

½ tbsp (8 ml) agave

Small pinch of salt

⅓ tsp tapioca

½ tsp lemon juice

Pinch of vanilla powder

Set out six small jars. To make the base, grind the almonds and oats in a food processor and add the salt, oil and syrup. Continue processing until a sticky dough is formed. I like keeping a bite to the base by leaving small bits of nuts in the crust; there's no need to get the dough completely smooth. Press the dough on the bottom of each jar. Place the jars in the freezer to chill while you prepare the other layers.

To prepare the chocolate, melt the oil in a double boiler, remove it and add the syrup. Stir until they're combined. Add the cocoa powder and keep stirring until smooth. Add the milk, salt and vanilla and continue mixing until it smooths and thickens into a melted-chocolate consistency. If it's too thick, add another tablespoon (15 ml) of milk. Divide the melted chocolate equally between the jars. Return them into the freezer to set while you make the vanilla cheesecake layer.

To make the vanilla cheesecake layer, wash and drain the cashews and place them in a high-speed blender. Add the lemon juice, syrup, vanilla, salt, ¼ cup (60 ml) of water and oil. Blend until the filling is completely smooth and creamy. If it is too thick to blend, add the rest of the reserved water gradually. Feel free to add more vanilla or syrup to taste.

Pour the filling on the chilled base and chocolate, shake the jars gently and tap them on the countertop to smooth the top and eliminate any air bubbles. Refrigerate again for at least 3 hours to set.

To prepare the strawberry coulis, place all the ingredients in the blender and blend until smooth. Pour it into a small saucepan and warm it over a low flame until boiling. Cook for a few minutes to thicken it. Remove the coulis from the flame, allow to cool completely and refrigerate for at least 1 hour.

After it is chilled, divide the coulis evenly between the jars and put them in the refrigerator to set for another hour; use as little or as much as you want. Serve the cheesecakes well chilled.

To store, cover each jar with a lid or plastic wrap and refrigerate for up to 1 week.

NOTES: To ensure these are gluten free, be sure to use certified gluten-free oats in the recipe.

I prefer using extra virgin coconut oil, but if you mind the taste of coconut, feel free to use odorless coconut oil.

KEY LIME MATCHA RAW CAKE

GLUTEN FREE; GRAIN FREE | YIELD: 1 (6-INCH [15-CM]) ROUND CAKE; 10 SLICES

I know that this is an American classic, but growing up in Croatia, I'd only recently heard of limes or matcha. It didn't take me long, though, to fall in love with this gorgeous tangy combination. One bite was enough.

BASE

1 cup (145 g) almonds

½ cup (75 g) peeled unsalted pistachios

Pinch of salt

½ cup (100 g) tightly packed, chopped pitted dates

1 tbsp (15 ml) melted extra virgin coconut oil (see Note)

1 tsp lime juice

½ tsp vanilla powder or 1 tsp vanilla extract

FILLING

2 cups (280 g) soaked cashews (see Note on page 16)

Pinch of salt

1 tsp psyllium husk

½ cup (120 ml) agave syrup, or more to taste

½ tsp vanilla powder

½ cup (120 ml) melted coconut oil

2 tsp (6 g) high-quality matcha powder

5 tbsp (75 ml) lime juice, about 2 limes

½ to ⅔ cup (120 to 160 ml) water

½ tsp matcha powder, optional to decorate

Line the bottom of a 6-inch (15-cm) round springform pan with parchment paper.

To make the base, roughly grind the almonds and pistachios and add the salt, dates, oil, lime juice and vanilla. Keep pulsing until you get a sticky dough.

Use a tablespoon to press and level the base, then push even more firmly and shape the edges using the flat bottom of a cup. Place it in the freezer until the filling is ready.

To prepare the filling, add the soaked cashews to the blender and add the salt, psyllium husk, syrup, vanilla, oil, matcha powder, lime juice and ½ cup (120 ml) of water. Blend until smooth. If the filling is too thick to blend, keep adding a little bit of reserved water until you can blend it into a perfectly smooth consistency. It is better to add as little water as possible, as the filling will be firmer once set. Pour it over the chilled base and shake the pan to smooth the top. Pat it gently on the countertop a few times to get the air bubbles out.

Cover it and refrigerate for at least 8 hours or overnight. If you're in a hurry, you can place the cake in the freezer for 5 to 6 hours to speed things up. It will become firmer as it is left for longer in the refrigerator. If you make this cake in advance and leave it to set and cool for at least 1 to 2 days, you will get perfectly sharp slices.

Slice and serve it straight out of the refrigerator. You can also decorate the cake by sifting some more matcha powder on top. It will keep in the refrigerator in a sealed container for up to 10 days. You can also freeze it for up to 4 months. To thaw, place it in the refrigerator for at least 30 to 45 minutes or 20 minutes at room temperature.

NOTE: I prefer using extra virgin coconut oil, but if you mind the taste of coconut, feel free to use odorless coconut oil.

PUFFED QUINOA CHOCOLATE BARS

GLUTEN FREE; GRAIN FREE | YIELD: 12 BARS

This kind of compact, chocolaty no-bake bar is my go-to quick bite when I need a little something as a pre- or post-workout snack or a quick dessert fix. I love how rich and decadent they taste while being such a nutritious and clean treat, loaded with healthy protein, fats, fibers and carbohydrates. They are also gluten and grain free, as quinoa isn't a grain but actually a seed. Often referred to as a pseudograin, these little gems are a true natural powerhouse that add amazing substance to these little bars.

BASE

⅔ cup (110 g) almonds

⅓ cup (45 g) roasted hazelnuts

½ cup (40 g) shredded coconut

2 pinches of salt

Pinch of vanilla powder

10 medium pitted and chopped dates, about ⅔ cup (110 g)

1 tbsp (30 g) almond butter

2 tbsp (30 ml) melted extra virgin coconut oil (see Note)

1 tbsp (15 ml) maple syrup

2 tbsp (20 g) unsweetened cocoa powder

1 tsp lemon juice

CHOCOLATE

4 tbsp (60 ml) melted extra virgin coconut oil

2 tbsp (30 ml) maple syrup

5 heaping tbsp (50 g) unsweetened cocoa powder

4 tbsp (60 ml) room temperature almond or oat milk

Pinch of salt

1 tbsp (30 g) plus 1 tsp almond butter (the runny kind), divided

½ heaping cup (20 g) plus 1 to 2 tsp (1 to 2 g) puffed quinoa, divided

Line a 9 x 5–inch (23 x 13–cm) pan with parchment paper, leaving the excess paper hanging over the long sides.

Place the almonds, hazelnuts, coconut, salt and vanilla in a food processor and blend into a coarse meal. Add the dates, almond butter, oil, syrup, cocoa powder and lemon juice. Keep pulsing until you get a sticky dough that sticks together when pinched in between your fingers. Press it firmly into the prepared pan and place it in the freezer to firm up while you make the chocolate.

To make the homemade chocolate, whisk the oil and syrup in a double boiler until melted, remove from the flame and add the cocoa powder. Keep whisking gently until it smooths out. Then gradually add the milk, the salt and 1 tablespoon (30 g) of almond butter, whisking until you get a smooth melted chocolate consistency.

Pour one-third of the prepared chocolate on the chilled base. Scatter the quinoa over it and pour the rest of the chocolate on top. Take a wooden spoon or a fork and swirl the chocolate and quinoa to mix. Shake the pan to coat the quinoa with chocolate and to level it. Optionally, you can swirl 1 teaspoon of almond butter on the surface and then scatter more quinoa as a decoration.

Refrigerate it for at least for 3 hours to set. When it is firmed up, use a sharp knife to slice it into bars and serve directly from the refrigerator.

Keep it in the refrigerator or freezer wrapped in plastic wrap, whole or cut in bars, in a closed container. They will keep in the refrigerator for up to 3 weeks, and they will keep for up to 4 months in the freezer. To serve, thaw them for at least 15 to 20 minutes at room temperature.

NOTE: I prefer using extra virgin coconut oil but if you mind the taste of coconut, feel free to use odorless coconut oil.

ACKNOWLEDGMENTS

I feel incredibly lucky to have been given the opportunity in life to share my passion with others and have this rewarding career. This is all thanks to all the amazing people who have followed and supported my Delicious & Healthy by Maya blog and Instagram account. So, my biggest thank you is to you.

I appreciate every like and comment. I appreciate you. I love getting your kind notes and photos of the successful recipe re-creations you made, telling me how I impacted your life and made you feel healthier and eat better and more deliciously. It always motivates me to do more and do better.

Secondly, thank you to my boyfriend, my amazing daughter, my family and my friends who have supported my work, patiently and enthusiastically tasting every single recipe that I made for this book. I apologize for making you eat all the desserts, but I'm sure you won't hold it against me.

And lastly, a huge thank you to my publisher Page Street Publishing and to the wonderful team that helped me through this process: especially my editor Jenna and creative director Meg. Jenna, your assistance and support were essential. Thank you.

ABOUT THE AUTHOR

Maja Brekalo is a best-selling cookbook author, writer and photographer behind the successful blog and Instagram Delicious & Healthy by Maya. She specializes in easy, fuss-free and wholesome plant-based recipes. Her first cookbook, *Moja sretna hrana (My Happy Food)*, published in her home country of Croatia, has quickly become a huge success even in non-vegan communities.

She is passionate about healthy, wholesome but also delicious food as well as educating people about environmental issues and promoting sustainability.

Maja is also a flight attendant and thinks she's incredibly lucky to be able to do two jobs she adores. She lives in Zagreb, Croatia, where she continues to create healthy, wholesome and delicious food and take beautiful photos every day.

Bake it Vegan is her first cookbook in English and her first dessert cookbook.

INDEX